According to John

The Witness of the Beloved Disciple

John F. O'Grady

PAULIST PRESS
New York / Mahwah, N.J.

Also by John F. O'Grady
published by Paulist Press

Disciples and Leaders
The Four Gospels and the Jesus Tradition
Models of Jesus Revisited
Pillars of Paul's Gospel
The Roman Catholic Church

Cover design by Bruce Crilly

Copyright © 1999 by John F. O'Grady

All rights reserved. No part of this book may be reproduced or transmitted in any form or by any means, electronic or mechanical, including photocopying, recording, or by any information storage and retrieval system without permission in writing from the Publisher.

Library of Congress Cataloging-in-Publication Data

O'Grady, John F.
    According to John : the witness of the beloved disciple / John F. O'Grady.
      p. cm.
    Includes index.
    ISBN 0–8091–3852–2 (alk. paper)
    1. Bible. N.T. John—Criticism, interpretation, etc. I. Title.
BS2615.2.035 1999
226.5′06—dc21   98–47602
                                                              CIP

Published by Paulist Press
997 Macarthur Boulevard
Mahwah, New Jersey 07430

www.paulistpress.com

Printed and bound in the
United States of America

Contents

Preface 1

I. THE GOSPEL OF JOHN

1. Jesus in the Gospel of John 7
Johannine Christology...The Prologue and the *Logos*
(Word)...The Son of Man...The Son of God...The Use
of *Ego Eimi* (I Am)...The Title *Logos*...The Son of
Man...Messiah/Christ

2. Individuals in the Gospel 20
Jesus...The Father...John the Baptist...Nathanael...
Nicodemus...The Samaritan Woman...The Royal Offi-
cial...The Lame Man and the Man Born Blind...
Philip...Martha, Mary and Lazarus...Judas...Mary, the
Mother of Jesus...Mary Magdalene...Thomas...
Peter...The Beloved Disciple

**3. Faith and Love: The Foundations of the
   Community** 39
Faith in the Fourth Gospel...Faith and God the
Father...Believing and Knowing...Individuals and
Faith...The Content of Faith...The Shepherd...The
Twofold Commandment...The One Commandment in
John...The Good Shepherd and the Vine and the
Branches...Johannine Mysticism...The Essentials of
Christianity

4. The Prologue 57
The Theology of the Word...The Origin of the *Logos*, the "Word"...Judaism and Philosophy...The Literary Structure

5. The Sacraments in the Fourth Gospel 67
Baptism...The Blind Man...The Foot Washing... Eucharistic Teaching...Faith and the Sacraments

6. The Farewell Discourses 82
The Command of Love...The Holy Spirit, the Paraclete...The Prayer of Jesus...Farewell Discourses in the Old Testament...The Prayer and the Eucharist...The High Priestly Prayer...Holiness...Unity...Final Glorification

7. The Passion of the Lord in the Fourth Gospel 93
Paul and the Synoptics...The Death of Jesus in the Fourth Gospel...The Passion of Jesus in the Four Gospels...The Passion in the Fourth Gospel...The Crucifixion...Jesus Reigns from the Cross

8. The Death of Jesus 102
Religious Experience...The Death of Jesus in the Fourth Gospel...The Revelation of God as Father...The Revelation in Jesus' Self-Offering...The Testimony of the Word, the Son...God Revealed in the Death of Jesus...God as Father

9. The Resurrection Appearances 110
The Resurrection in the Synoptics...Individuals and Places Associated with the Resurrection...Resurrection Appearances in the Fourth Gospel...Jesus and His Friends

II. THE JOHANNINE COMMUNITY AND THEOLOGY

10. The Eschatology of the Fourth Gospel 121
Future and Present Eschatology...Salvation is *NOW*... Eternal Life...Judgment in the Present...Resurrection on the Last Day...Eschatology and the Individual Believer...The Future Assured

11. The Community Behind the Fourth Gospel 129
The "Johannine School"...Groups Within the Community...Problems in the Community...Johannine Dualism...Gnosticism and Qumran...Christology

12. The Beloved Disciple 140
Identity...The Origin of the Passages...The Inspirer of
the Gospel...Methodology...Historicity...Phenomenol-
ogy and Anthropology...The Community of the Beloved
Disciple and the Beloved Disciple

13. The Gospel According to John Today 150
Individualism...Individual and Community in John...
Faith, Love and Good Order...Personal Faith Commit-
ment...Sacraments...Love in the Community...The One
Word of God

Appendix: A Thematic Guide to the Gospel of John 160

Selected Bibliography 169

Index 171

For
John Francis O'Grady, II
and
John Francis O'Grady, III

Preface

M any students and in fact many adults studying the Bible find
reading a commentary on a particular book of the Bible tedious.
They do not mind studying one or two verses and seeing what many
commentators say about them but do not want to have to do the
same for all of the verses of a particular book. They seem to learn
more about the book and more quickly when they have a general
understanding of the book in question and then read it from beginning to end. In this way they feel more comfortable with the ideas
contained therein.

This book responds to that need of students. I do not offer a
verse by verse commentary. Instead I offer a general approach to
the gospel of John that should help readers and students appreciate
the full gospel. Picking out little sections and then encouraging
someone to read the whole gospel creates a sense of knowing some
of the characters and some of the basic thought.

Studying Jesus and the large number of individuals who move
in and out of the drama of this gospel helps readers to identify with
what they read. They get a good sense of who Jesus is in this gospel
and then also appreciate the people around Jesus. The diversity of
approaches both to Jesus and the many individuals singled out in
the gospel adds an interest that should cause a desire for further
understanding. Students or readers can also begin to see how the
understanding of Jesus, who he was and what he did, continues to
influence people today.

Some chapters seem better suited to more detailed analysis
than others. I have chosen the prologue to the gospel and some sections of chapter seventeen for this type of analysis. I trust my reasons will become evident.

Throughout this work I have avoided referring to the author

as John. No one really knows who wrote the gospel or who was responsible for it. I believe that someone known as the Beloved Disciple stands behind the witness to this gospel, but he remains an unknown disciple. This gospel will still be called the Gospel According to John, but even John is relatively unknown in the early church. Who wrote it or inspired it matters little. What is truly historical and what is the creation of the evangelist also matters little. The story counts. Not only is the story powerful—it fascinates.

I expect readers and students to read the pertinent passages as they are presented. I also hope when the study is over readers will read the gospel from beginning to end at one sitting several times. Perhaps they may choose to use the appendix as a help. Once someone does this, the gospel of John becomes a companion for a lifetime.

For more than twenty years I have studied and loved this gospel. Each time I read it, I see verses I never saw before. It continues to fascinate and teach me. Over these years I have benefited from the work of others, in particular Raymond Brown, S.S., Rudolph Schnackenburg and Raymond Collins from my own tradition and have learned much from Robert Kysar and J. Louis Martyn from the Protestant tradition. I also must acknowledge Rudolph Bultmann, the famous German Lutheran exegete who constantly reminded me, through his writings, of the lack of certainty for many positions presented in the past and the need to relate the gospel to the lives of believers.

Over the years I have written frequently on this gospel. Many of the ideas in this book have appeared in *Biblical Theology Bulletin, Chicago Studies,* my short book *The Gospel of John* and the section on this gospel in my book *The Four Gospels and the Jesus Tradition.* Here for the first time I have tried to pull these many thoughts together coherently. At the same time this work is new. It shows the development of my own thought over this period of time.

Doris H. Barrage of Barry University helped me with several computer problems in creating this book. I extend my gratitude to her. The people of St. Matthew's Parish in Voorheesville, New York, allowed me peace and quiet with occasional time for fun while writing most of this. Many of these parishioners I have known for more than twenty-five years. They too have listened to me as I preached on this gospel and have responded by growing to love it as I do. My gratitude to them remains a constant in my life.

John is a great name. I feel privileged to bear it. At birth I was given another name by my father. But before my baptism my mother also said: "He shall be called John." Thank God my mother prevailed and my father gave in. My nephew also bears this name as does his son. And so someone named John writes a book about the Gospel According to John in honor of all those named John, but especially the two who are most dear to me.

Voorheesville, New York
July 1997
Miami, Florida
August 1997

■ PART I ■

The Gospel of John

1.

Jesus in the Gospel of John

S ometime toward the end of the first century a Christian community created the Gospel According to John. Who they were, where they lived, who their founder and inspiration was lie buried in the history of the early church. How long they survived as a Christian community also remains unknown. Like the life of any community something came and went as people came and went. But these individual believers in Jesus lived their faith with a zeal and a staunch sense of their place in history. They accepted Jesus and told his story as they wanted to tell it. The story has never disappeared.

Each gospel records the life, ministry, passion, death and resurrection of Jesus. His work and person form the heart of the gospel. But the gospel of John presents Jesus in a different manner from Matthew, Mark and Luke. These latter gospels have the name synoptics precisely because they portray Jesus in a similar way, differing considerably from the fourth and last written gospel. The gospels of Matthew, Mark and Luke devote much time to the ministry of Jesus, with emphasis on miracles and parables. The author of the Fourth Gospel devotes little time to miracles and narrates only two parables. In contrast to the synoptics, the author adds long discourses by Jesus relatively, but not totally, unknown in the other gospel traditions.

■ Johannine Christology ■

Scholars have frequently studied the picture of Jesus in this gospel searching for the key to unlock the meaning and purpose of this distinctive approach. They have studied the various titles used for Jesus, the interplay between the human and the divine Jesus, the interaction of who Jesus was and what he did. Many concluded by offering their key to help understand Jesus in this gospel. Although many keys have been offered, none ever seems adequate. Perhaps the christology of John relates to his anthropology. Or perhaps the key to understanding Jesus in this gospel is discovered by the reader in a more personal manner. Johannine approaches to Jesus and his meaning must always include the understanding of people of faith who come to believe in Jesus.

> These are written that you may believe that Jesus is the messiah, the Son of God, so that through this faith you may have life in his name (20:31).

But can anyone really identify with the Jesus of this gospel? Even a cursory reading of the gospel forces the reader to recognize a very divine Jesus. It begins with a hymn celebrating the pre-existent Word of God, related to God with a closeness of persons: "The Word was with God and the Word was God"(1:1). The Word certainly became flesh, became human, as Son, but never left the bosom of the Father: "The only Son, who is in the bosom of the Father, has made him known" (1:18). Jesus of Nazareth, the Word become flesh, moreover, possessed supernatural knowledge (1:48; 4:17–18); he cured with a word (4:50), changed water into wine (2:7–9), gave life through his word to Lazarus (11:43). He never suffered. With a serenity that astonished all, he controlled his passion from the moment of arrest to his final proclamation that it is finished.

The Divinity of Jesus

The contrast to the synoptics makes evident the emphasis on the divinity of Jesus in this gospel. In the earlier gospels Jesus does not know everything. He grows in wisdom and grace (Lk 2:52); he appears to be ignorant of the final day (Mk 13:32); he suffers painful agony (Lk 22:40–42) and he cries from the cross: "My God my God, why have you abandoned me?" (Mk 15:34). Jesus experiences temptation in the synoptics (Mt 4:1–11; Lk 4:1–13) and appears defeated by the power of evil in his death. Most people look to the synoptics to study the human Jesus, and they study the divine Jesus in the gospel of John. In fact, however, the Fourth Gospel portrays *both* the human and the divine Jesus, even if one seems much more evident.

■ The Prologue and the *Logos* (Word) ■

The origin and meaning of the title *Logos* in the prologue of this gospel has generated an immense amount of literature over the centuries. The author uses the title only in the prologue, although the theology of the "Word of God" dominates the gospel. The author seized upon a term used in both Jewish and Hellenistic circles and used it as his instrument to set forth a part of the Jesus tradition. The theology of the title is broader than its use in the first chapter. Jesus *is* the Word of God, and thus when he speaks, he reveals God. The words of Jesus, God his father has taught him (8:40; 14:10, 24). The content of this Word from God the Father concerns the person of Jesus and his relationship to God the Father and to the disciples. As Word, he reveals the Father and invites individuals to respond to this revelation. The prologue itself clearly emphasizes the divinity of Jesus. The Word pre-exists, functions in creation, gives light and life, reveals the glory of God through the manifestation of grace and truth, and returns to the Father from whose side he has never left. The reader can easily picture a divine person with God, descending upon this earth to fulfill a mission and then returning. The Word is divine; Jesus is divine.

■ The Son of Man ■

The title Son of Man appears in all four gospels. The use in John's gospel, however, differs significantly from the use in the synoptics. The evangelist focuses on the pre-existence of the Son of Man as well as his exaltation and glorification. The stress lies on the divine. The author uses the title as a characteristic self-designation. The idea in the background seems to be a figure who is archetype of the human race. The Johannine Son of Man descended from heaven and will ascend again. No one has ascended into heaven but he who descended from heaven, the Son of Man (3:13). "Then what if you were to see the Son of Man ascending where he was before?" (6:62). Jesus, as Son of Man, continues his union with God and dwells with God. He is the perfect one, the archetype who epitomizes the true and ultimate relationship of individuals with God. His heavenly origin is the basis for his ultimate elevation and glorification as well as his salvific activity. God the Father has already set his seal on the Son of Man (6:27), and from the Father he has received his transcendent message (3:11–13). This becomes the guarantee of his future return (6:62). The title carries a sense of pre-existence; when people encounter the Son of Man on earth, they face a divine being.

■   The Son of God   ■

The title Son of God does not appear often in this gospel. The original conclusion to the gospel in chapter 20 states that it was written to help individuals to believe that "Jesus is the Christ the Son of God" (20:31); it appears in the opening chapter, spoken by Nathanael (1:49); and it appears in the trial before Pilate (19:7). Jesus is the Son of God because God sanctified him and sent him into this world for a mission. But since the title can be used for other divine emissaries, it need not denote divinity. The close relationship between Jesus and God is better expressed in the use of "Son."

Jesus as Son

Jesus is God's Son. For the author of the Fourth Gospel this designated the close relationship between Jesus and God. The Son does only what he sees the Father doing:

> The Son can do nothing of his own accord, but only what
> he sees the Father doing, for whatever he does, that the
> Son does likewise (5:19).

Such examples stress the dependence of the Son upon the Father, but other texts imply equality. The Son, like the Father, gives life (5:21); the Son makes people free (8:36); the Son gives eternal life (3:36; 6:40) and the Father has given judgment to the Son (5:22). The Son seems to stand in equality with God and often cannot be completely distinguished from God the Father.

The Son Belongs to the Divine World

The Son lives in the divine world and receives all from the Father (5:20; 8:47).

> He who comes from above is above all; he who is of the
> earth belongs to the earth, and of the earth he speaks; he
> who comes from heaven is above all. He bears witness to
> what he has seen and heard (3:31–32).

All that the Son reveals depends on his previous participation in the divine world. The Son has pre-existed in the divine world as the Word and reveals what he had learned from God his Father in this world.

The Son as Divine Being

For the author of this gospel, speaking about a pre-existence is not sufficient to understand the Son. He gives divine prerogatives to the human Jesus. As Jesus knows things supernaturally, he also prays differently:

> "Father, I thank you that you have heard me. I knew that you hear me always, but I have said this on account of the people standing by" (11:41–42).

Instead of fearing death, as in the synoptics, when facing death Jesus offers a prayer glorifying the divine name (12:27–28). As divine, even his captors fall down before him (18:6). The title Son of God may not signify a divine being, but when this title is joined to "Son," the readers of this gospel learn the intention of the author to teach belief in a divine being.

■   The Use of *Ego Eimi* (I Am)   ■

The study of *ego eimi* (I am) has also generated a wealth of material. The author used the expression nine times throughout the gospel. When Jesus used the expression in the gospel he addressed a variety of audiences. Only one other individual uses the expression. The blind man responds with the expression *ego eimi* when the bystanders question his identity (9:9). This example differs from all the other times the phrase appears and helps clarify the meaning. On the lips of the blind man, the expression can mean "I am the one." In the past some dismissed these sayings by Jesus as of little consequence using this meaning. More recently scholars have viewed the expression as a theophonic formula representing the divine name or presence.

Source for the Phrase *Ego Eimi*

Several possibilities can explain the origin of the phrase. Some claim it comes from Hellenism, others that it comes from the Jewish tradition in which *ego eimi* is the Greek translation for the Hebrew expression *ani hu* found in Deutero-Isaiah, as well as the Jewish practice to substitute *ani hu* for the sacred name *YHWH.* The latter opinion seems to make more sense. The phrase *ani hu* occurs six times in Isaiah 40–55. The translators of the Hebrew text into Greek (LXX or Septuagint) chose the Greek expression *ego eimi* to translate *ani hu.* Isaiah uses the phrase to signify that *YHWH* alone is God. It presents *YHWH* as the Lord of history and creator of the world, closely related to other expressions of divine self-predication, especially the phrase, "I am *YHWH.*" In Jewish liturgical practice the words *I* or *He,* by themselves, were sometimes used as surrogates for the sacred name. The expression *ani hu* was used in the liturgy of the feast of Tabernacles, and the expression also appears in commentaries on the Passover service.

The Purpose of the "I Am" Phrase in John

The author seems to have selected this terminology to indicate the close relationship between Jesus and God as well as to indicate that a new age has dawned by his presence:

> "I tell you this now, before it takes place, so that when it takes place you may believe that *ego eimi*" (13:19).

Jesus answered them:

> "I solemnly declare it, before Abraham came to be, *ego eimi*" (8:58).

These examples admit of no predicate understood in context. They first can be compared with Isaiah 43:10:

> "You are my witnesses," says the LORD, "my servants whom I have chosen, to know and believe in me and understand that I am. Before me no god was formed, and after me there shall be none."

The author underlines the solemnity of the statement by Jesus. Only he could make it, and only those who believe in him could understand its meaning.

The second example helps in the further disclosure of the meaning of the phrase. When the Jews heard *ego eimi,* "they took up stones to throw at him"(8:59). A similar reaction appears in chapter

10:22–39. Jesus is in the temple and proclaims: "I and the Father are one" (v. 30). The reaction is the same: he has blasphemed and they seek to stone him. The use of *ego eimi* stresses the unity of Father and Son, God and Jesus.

Implied Reference

Other examples of the use of this phrase admit of a predicate understood. The phrase when used in the Garden of Olives shocks the reader. The soldiers, with Judas, approach Jesus and his band of disciples. Jesus maintains complete control and asks:

> "Who is it you want?" "Jesus the Nazarene," they replied. *Ego eimi,* he answered. Now Judas, the one who was to hand him over, was there with them. As Jesus said to them, *ego eimi,* they retreated slightly and fell to the ground....."I have told you, *ego eimi,*" Jesus said. "If I am the one you want, let these men go"(18:4–6, 8).

English translators usually choose to add the pronoun "he," translating the phrase "I am he." The Greek phrase is just *ego eimi,* I am. The context can presume the meaning, "I am the one." But when Jesus said *ego eimi,* they retreated and fell down. In the presence of the divine, the only appropriate reaction is adoration.

Only one example in the gospel of John finds a parallel in the synoptics. When Jesus comes to his disciples by walking on the sea he announces: "It is I *(ego eimi),* do not be afraid" (Mk 6:50; Mt 14:27). In Deutero-Isaiah *ani hu* occurs sometimes in association with the power of God over creation, especially his power over the sea. Earlier people often looked upon the sea as an abode of evil spirits, anxious to destroy all who ventured out too far. This may underlie the usage in Mark and Matthew. Perhaps this was the source of the theology used by the author of the Fourth Gospel in his use of the phrase.

Conclusion of *Ego Eimi*

The evangelist uses the phrase in an absolute sense in 8:58 and 13:19. The phrase centers on the divine presence in Jesus. People must recognize the unity between God and Jesus. When

Jesus spoke: "Before Abraham was, *ego eimi*" (8:58), his listeners and readers today should retreat in awe in the presence of the divine.

The Humanity of Jesus

The image of Jesus portrayed in the Fourth Gospel certainly differs significantly from that in the other gospels. Jesus is the eternal Word of God, the heavenly Son of Man, the Son of God. He alone represents the presence of the eternal God. He appears so divine in outlook that Christians for centuries have used this gospel to preach the divinity of Jesus and often have overlooked the humanity of Jesus presented therein. No one can deny the emphasis on the divinity of Jesus in this gospel. But to fail to see how this same Jesus is also very human does an injustice to the genius of the Johannine community, its theology and the individuals responsible for the gospel. This gospel portrays a human Jesus as well as the divine Jesus.

Although the Word existed for all eternity with God the Father, no hint at a supernatural origin for Jesus appears in this gospel. Matthew and Luke offer the infancy stories about Jesus and both imply that the origin of Jesus was unlike any other human origin: Jesus was virginally conceived. This gospel, in contrast, refers to Jesus as the son of Joseph:

> We have found the one about whom Moses wrote in the law, and about whom the prophets spoke, I mean Jesus, the son of Joseph, the man from Nazareth (1:45).

> They kept saying, "Is this not Jesus, the son of Joseph, whose father and mother we know?" (6:42).

Jesus belongs to a particular family and, unlike Mark who refers to Jesus as the son of Mary (Mk 6:3), John calls him the son of Joseph. Chapter 8 offers some evidence that perhaps Joseph was not the father of Jesus. In fact, Jesus was illegitimate. While Jesus debates the Jews, he makes reference to God his Father and they reply, "Where is your father?" (8:19). The accusation becomes clearer as the debate continues. In reply to Jesus' accusation that the Jews do the work of their father, the devil, they reply, "We were not born of an adulterous union" (8:41). Some saw Jesus as the son of Joseph and Mary; others conclude that somehow he was illegitimate. Perhaps Jesus was born within the first nine-month period that Mary and

Joseph lived as husband and wife. The followers of Jesus concluded that Jesus' origin was divine intervention; others thought he was born out of wedlock. The author of the Fourth Gospel chose to record the impression of the latter while also maintaining that Jesus was the son of Joseph and yet divine.

Jesus: His Friends and His Needs

Jesus needed human affection. One of his disciples intimately leans on his breast at the Last Supper (13:25); he loved Martha and Mary and Lazarus (11:5); he spent time with his mother and brothers and even attended a marriage celebration (2:1–11). On his journey to Samaria he grew tired and thirsty (4:6). Like thousands before him and after him, he stopped at Jacob's Well to rest and receive refreshment. He changed his mind. When the disciples asked him if he intended to go to Jerusalem for the feast of Tabernacles, he declined (7:8). Then he changed his mind and went (7:10). He does not experience a painful agony in the garden in this gospel or temptation in the desert. The author preserves some hint at these aspects of his life, however, when he remarks:

> "I am troubled now. Yet what should I say? 'Father, save me from this hour.' But it was for this purpose that I came to this hour" (12:27).

He shows emotion frequently:

> When Jesus saw her weeping, and when he saw the Jews who had come with her weeping, he was deeply moved in spirit so that an involuntary groan burst from him and he trembled with deep emotion (11:33).

> Jesus said to them: "Where have you laid him?" "Lord" they said to him, "come and see."... Jesus wept (11:34–35).

> "Now my soul is troubled" (12:27).

> When Jesus had said these things, he was troubled in spirit (13:21).

The first examples display the emotion of Jesus as he encounters his friends after the death of Lazarus. The human Jesus sorrows at the death of a friend. The divine Jesus utters a word, and Lazarus comes forth. The next examples contain fear and anxiety. He knows he will die, but instead of seeking release he gladly accepts the will of God. Jesus appears happy in the presence of good friends. He knows bodily needs. He also knows fear and anxiety as he faces death and even experiences the depression of someone betrayed by a friend. Jesus is very human in this gospel.

■   **The Title** *Logos*   ■

Many of the titles used by this evangelist connote a divine being. Some display subtle hints that the divinity of Jesus was never separated from his humanity. *Logos* emphasizes divinity, but *Logos* becomes flesh. The climax of the hymn in the prologue is the relationship between *Logos* and flesh. The *Logos* entered into the human and earthly sphere. Before *Logos* was in the glory of God; now *Logos* has taken on the lowliness of human existence. In Johannine terms flesh *(sarkx)* means the earthbound, as seen in 3:6; it connotes the transient and perishable, as seen in 6:63. Flesh is the typical mode of being human in contrast to the divine and the spiritual. The use of this word need not connote some reference to the sacrifice of the Lord, "my flesh for the life of the world" (6:51), but it might be in the mind of the evangelist. The prologue contains many of the principal themes of the gospel. The reader might expect this central point of Johannine theology to figure here as well. If the use of this word makes even a veiled reference to the death of Jesus, this brings a further indication of the relationship between the *Logos* and human existence, destined to death. The flesh assumed by the *Logos* is the presupposition for the death on the cross. Once the *Logos* becomes flesh, the author no longer used *Logos* as a title in the gospel, for in the humanity of Jesus people have contact with the divine.

■   **The Son of Man**   ■

The Fourth Gospel frequently contains double-meaning words with various levels of thought. The title Son of Man translates the Hebrew *ben adam,* a variant of the Aramaic *bar e nas* or *bar a nasa.* Recent studies have shown these expressions can mean "everyman" or "anyone." Son of Man can designate the ideal person or the ordinary person. Mark used this expression in 2:27–28. Matthew also knows this meaning, for he changed Mark's "sons of men" to just "men" (Mt 12:31). Matthew knew that *sons of men* is generic for *men* just as *son of man* is generic for *man* or *everyman*. The evangelist surely knew the Aramaic idiom and was capable of linguistic subtlety. The author of the gospel was also fond of using "man" in reference to Jesus when other more honorific titles could have been used:

> "Who is the man who said to you, 'lift up your bed and walk?'" (5:12).

> "You, a man, make yourself God" (10:33).

> "It is better that one man should die for the people, rather than the whole nation should perish" (11:50).

> The maid servant who kept the door said to Peter: "Are you not this man's disciple?" (18:17).

> So Pilate came out to them and said: "What accusation do you bring against this man?" (18:29).

> "Behold the man" (19:5).

The Son of Man has a heavenly origin; he possesses divine characteristics. He is also everyman, a man like anyone else. He epitomizes the best in human nature, and in him people discover the divine reality. Jesus is Son of God like other faithful messengers with a divine mission. He is Son as well, implying a divine existence with God his Father. The human dimension of his Sonship, however, appears evident in two passages.

> "He who believes in me, believes not in me but in him who sent me. And he who sees me sees him who sent me" (12:44–45).

> "Have I been with you so long, Philip, and you do not know me? He who sees me sees the Father" (14:9).

Jesus reveals the Father because he is the Son. Look upon the humanity of Jesus and see the God of all. The Son reveals the Father in human flesh, for people learn only humanly. If God chooses to reveal, God must do so humanly. The Son revealed the Father by being a human Son.

The Use of *Ego Eimi* as a Title

The unusual use of *ego eimi* relates Jesus to the divine. The author of this gospel, however, also used this phrase with predicates. Jesus said: "I am the bread of life" (6:35); "the light of the world" (8:12); "the door" (10:7); "the good shepherd" (10:11); "the resurrection and the life" (11:25); "the way, and the truth, and the life" (14:6); "the true vine" (15:1). Such self-presentations appear in the Old Testament (Dt 32; Sir 24) as well as in other Ancient Near Eastern texts. Often *ego eimi* connotes the care the deity has for the created order. The author of this gospel added qualifying adjectives: Jesus is the "good" shepherd, the "true" vine and light. All such predicates and adjectives relate Jesus to human life. As *ego eimi* Jesus is divine; he is also light to people; he is truth and the way, offering guidance and direction; Jesus is bread and the vine that sustains the branches, both offering life. He is the door through which people enter to find security; he is the shepherd who provides nourishment and protection from evil. Finally, Jesus is the resurrection, which promises eternal life. Again, the author moves from the divine level to the human level with his use of *ego eimi*. When Jesus proclaims: "Before Abraham came to be, *ego eimi*" (8:58), the reader faces the divine; when he says he is bread and light and truth, his followers know the divine has come humanly.

■   Messiah/Christ   ■

The title Messiah or Christ refers primarily to the humanity of Jesus. The gospel opens with a confession that Jesus is the messiah: "We have found the Messiah" (1:41). The set purpose of the gospel in John 20:31 includes belief in Jesus as messiah. Throughout the gospel, however, the title implies a spiritual reality rather than a political reality. In several passages in the Old Testament Wisdom replaces the role of the messiah. In their zeal for the Law, some scribes even began to identify the Law with Wisdom. The two parallel movements converge on Jesus. A prophetic tradition saw salvation and redemption as God's work through a messiah in history. Wisdom literature depicted salvation and redemption already implanted in creation by God. Individuals who live according to their consciences would discover Wisdom and experience the saving presence of God. The former movement centered on the external, the latter on the internal. Both concepts are united in the Fourth Gospel. Jesus is Incarnate Wisdom. People can look at him and discover the

Wisdom God has implanted in the universe. Jesus fulfills the Law and prophets and is Wisdom Incarnate. The title *Christ* focuses on humanity that expresses divinity. Jesus as the incarnation of Wisdom bears the divine. He cannot be the messiah unless individuals see a human being who releases all of the possible energies implanted in humanity by a provident God. When the evangelist claims that Jesus is the Messiah, the Christ, he proclaims the human Jesus can lead to the divine both by fulfilling the prophets and expressing Wisdom.

Conclusion

The Fourth Gospel has long been recognized as emphasizing the divinity of Jesus. It also preserves his humanity. It does not, however, resolve the relationship between the two. The Johannine community preserved a particular sensitivity to the divinity of Jesus but would not fall into the mistaken notion that the divinity eclipsed the humanity. With careful progression the author led from humanity to divinity without losing anything in the process. The divine Jesus of the Fourth Gospel is the very human Jesus of Nazareth.

Suggestions for Reflection

1. Jesus is the "Word of God." What does this expression mean to you and how can this expression help you to understand better the mission of Jesus?
2. The title Son of Man can connote divinity. It also can emphasize humanity. How does this affect your understanding of Jesus and yourself?
3. Jesus is God's Son. This title is more important than Son of God. What implications can you see in this title for contemporary Christians?
4. The use of "I am" is unusual in this gospel. After studying all of the times it is used, what are your thoughts?
5. Jesus was never a political messiah. Would you prefer him to be understood politically today? How can he be a messiah if he is not involved with the political and social aspects of human life?
6. How do you relate humanity and divinity in your own life, and how has this been affected by your study of the gospel of John?

2.

Individuals in the Gospel

■ Jesus ■

*J*esus reveals God. Jesus is God's human face. Individuals in the Fourth Gospel respond by faith to the revelation of Jesus. The acceptance is active; a decision must be made. When Jesus enters into a person's life, the individual has the opportunity to lose any illusions and accept the offered salvation. The true believer accepts Jesus not just as a miracle worker or a great teacher or a good guide in the complexity of life but precisely as the Son of God, the one who makes God known. Accept—or reject—even if the acceptance is not always perfect.

■ The Father ■

In this process God the Father of Jesus plays a significant role. No movement to faith is possible without the presence of God. The God and Father of Jesus gives the disciples to Jesus and actually teaches them through Jesus. Individual believers and nonbelievers in this gospel become representative figures. The author chose various persons from the common gospel tradition or selected others from his own tradition to illustrate some point about the nature of faith, its presence or absence, and the person's relationship to Jesus. These individuals are not merely figments of the writer's imagination, nor are they described in a completely historical way. Rather, they often have a historical foundation but are presented in a peculiarly Johannine way to teach the evangelist's readers or audience something about the faith in Jesus that gives life.

■ John the Baptist ■

Please read John 1:6–8, 15, 19–34; 3:22–30; 4:1–3; 5:33–36; 10:40–42.

The introductory narrative about John the Baptist (1:19–34) is followed by another scene in which John appears (3:22–30). Two rather problematic sections in the first chapter (1:6–8, 15 and 4:1–3) may be the work of an editor who inserted these verses to counteract the influence of John on some contemporaries of the evangelist. In two other passages in later chapters Jesus also speaks of John (5:33–36; 10:40–41).

John the Baptizer in the Fourth Gospel differs considerably from the John presented in the synoptics. To begin with, the synoptics refer to him as the "Baptizer." In the Fourth Gospel he is never so designated. He is simply John. Surely the readers knew that John baptized, but the activity is not introduced until verse 25.

The John of the Fourth Gospel is a John of Christian faith. He has come to bear testimony to the light; he has accepted Jesus and then become his witness. He confesses that Jesus is the lamb of God (1:29) and he on whom the Spirit remains (1:32). His representative role figures in the verse that stands as the climax of the first appearance of the Baptist: "I have seen for myself and have testified, 'This is God's chosen One'" (1:34).

John came from God. God sent him to recognize the presence of the Spirit in Jesus and confess that Jesus is the Son of God. The author of this gospel does not choose to emphasize John's role in baptizing. John represents the first example of the fulfillment of Johannine christology in a confessing believer. He has seen and believed and testified.

The author contrasts Jesus and John. John baptizes in water; Jesus baptizes in the spirit. Jesus has more followers than John and more are baptized in the Spirit, although Jesus himself does not baptize (4:1–3). John bears witness to the light but is not the light (1:6–8). Jesus is the light. Jesus proclaims that John was a bright and shining lamp (5:35), but the testimony of Jesus is greater than the lamp of John (5:36). Nor did John perform signs as Jesus did (10:40–42).

The presence of John in the Fourth Gospel represents the true follower of Jesus who recognizes that the Spirit of God has descended and remained on Jesus (1:32). Once John has come to see in Jesus the presence of the Spirit of God, he has no choice but to render testimony to others. He points out Jesus for others as he himself has discovered the presence of God in Jesus. John is the first believer in this gospel. His task no longer means preaching and baptizing but merely pointing to the Jesus he has personally accepted as the lamb of God and the one on whom the Spirit of God remains. Two of the disciples of John accompany their master when he sees Jesus walk by. John points to Jesus and the two disciples leave John to follow Jesus (1:35–37).

■ Nathanael ■

Please read John 1:43–51; 21:2.

Nathanael appears only in the Johannine tradition. His first appearance occurs in the call of the first disciples (1:43–51), and he reappears in the final chapter with the other disciples as they go fishing. The first appearance can be viewed as a transformed vocation scene. The conversation between Jesus and Nathanael seems somewhat contrived in order to lead to the great testimony by Nathanael: "You are the Son of God; you are the king of Israel" (1:49).

This disciple represents the true Israelite who comes to faith in Jesus. The author describes him as a man seated "under the fig tree." To a perceptive reader this recalls the Jewish tradition about the study of the scriptures under the fig tree. No greater enjoyment and sense of peace can be found than sitting under a fig tree with food and shade and, of necessity, water nearby, studying the word of God. Jesus reveals God and perceives the incipient faith in a man who bears an Old Testament name and engages in activity most characteristic of God's people. The author actually uses a technical formula for revelation, identifying Nathanael as an "Israelite. There is no guile in him" (1:47).

Nathanael responds with a profession of personal faith and calls Jesus the "king of Israel," a traditional messianic title (Mk 15:32). To this confession the evangelist adds the additional confession "Son of God." This title brings the confession in accord with the christology of the gospel, which sees Jesus as the messiah because he is God's Son, not in the Old Testament sense of one specially chosen, but in the typically Johannine sense of the one who has a unique relationship with God the Father. Many can be God's Son but only Jesus can be the Son who knows God so intimately.

Nathanael had searched the scriptures and had come to believe in Jesus and made his personal commitment to him. He has no need to ask Jesus, "Who are you?" Nathanael will learn who

Jesus is because Jesus has called him the true Israelite. He receives the answer to his unasked question: Jesus is the Son of Man (1:51). This verse may have been added to the Nathanael episode at a later stage of the development of the gospel tradition. Its presence, however, contributes to the theology of the gospel not only because of the meaning of the title Son of Man, but because the title makes Nathanael the first bearer of a formula that presents Jesus as both the Son of God and Son of Man. Nathanael has responded personally to the revelation of Jesus as both titles imply. He represents faithful followers of the traditions of Israel who see in Jesus their fulfillment. Jesus reveals God in a human way.

■ Nicodemus ■

Please read John 3:1–15; 7:45–52; 19:38–42.

The episode of Nicodemus coming to Jesus at night exemplifies an imperfect coming to faith. Jesus impressed Nicodemus, and so Nicodemus calls Jesus Master (3:2). He apparently belongs to a group of people drawn to Jesus because of his miracles, but he is also one who goes beyond the mere miraculous: "No man can perform signs and wonders such as you perform unless God is with him" (3:2). This faith, however, apparently remains insufficient. Nicodemus may represent people of good will who also may be leaders in Judaism but have difficulties in accepting Jesus. The foreboding of Jesus in verses 11 and 12 cannot be forgotten: the individual may come to Jesus impressed by signs but must be drawn by the Father to Jesus in order to accept Jesus in faith.

Scholars disagree on many aspects of this dialogue. Of particular note is the discussion on the discourse by Jesus. Is it from Jesus or is it a speech created by the evangelist? Also, where does the dialogue between Jesus and Nicodemus end, and is the discourse then continued by Jesus or by the teaching of the evangelist? Some hold for a break after verse 12, with the rest a kerygmatic discourse by the evangelist. Others see the break after verse 16. The best position seems to be to accept the chapter as written, without any effort to delineate its origins or its composition.

The entire discourse seems to be a condensation of the principal assertions of Johannine theology and therefore comes from the teaching of the community. Jesus, having been sent by the Father, reveals the Father. Jesus accomplishes this full revelation and redemption on the cross. The author refers to the death of Jesus cryptically in the reference to being lifted up so that those who believe may have eternal life (3:14–15). On the part of the individual, Jesus offers a summons that demands a personal decision actually accomplished through the power of God.

Perhaps the original episode between Jesus and Nicodemus was part of the Jesus tradition known to the community of John, but this gave rise to a fuller theology of coming to faith in Jesus. Probably the author joins some legitimate remembrances of Jesus' teaching to a historical episode, but the teaching need not be tied irrevocably to an encounter between Jesus and Nicodemus. It is the theological meaning that remains primary: some individuals, even of good faith and of sufficient knowledge, experience difficulties in accepting Jesus. They need the powerful assistance of God in order to come to faith in Jesus.

Nicodemus returns on two other occasions in this gospel. In 7:50 he again appears as one who is interested in Jesus, or at least curious, and he believes that Jesus is being mistreated by the Pharisees. When his fellow Pharisees condemn Jesus, Nicodemus reminds them: "Since when does our law condemn any man without first hearing him and knowing the facts?" (7:51). When Nicodemus encounters further opposition, he remains silent.

Finally, he returns for the third and last time after the death of Jesus. In 19:38–42 he joins Joseph of Arimathea and buries Jesus. Some see in this episode the final coming to faith by Nicodemus. But the author makes no mention of faith. Nicodemus performs a kindness for Jesus in assisting in his burial. This need not flow from a personal faith commitment.

Nicodemus seems to represent all those good people who for one reason or another never come to full faith in Jesus. He was curious, recognizes that God was with Jesus, defends him publicly against the Pharisees and assists in his burial. Is this enough for faith? Are these actions expressions of faith? Whatever the fate of the historical Nicodemus, he bears witness in this gospel to the problems of believing even for good people. If God does not draw, people cannot see the face of God in Jesus of Nazareth.

■   The Samaritan Woman   ■

Please read John 4:1–42.

The coming to faith by the Samaritan woman and her profession of Jesus as the messiah contrast sharply with the searchers for miracles in the second chapter of John:

> Now when he was in Jerusalem at the Passover feast
> many believed in his name when they saw the signs
> which he did but Jesus did not trust himself to them
> (2:23–24).

The Samaritan woman also draws into focus the reaction of Nicodemus, a leader of the people, in contrast to her own openness, and even the suspicious attitude of the Pharisees in John 9:13. Jesus gives living water, reveals true worship, and offers salvation. The Samaritan woman accepted the words of Jesus even if she did not fully understand. Moreover, the woman not only came to faith but became a missionary, bringing others to Jesus.

> The woman said to him, "Sir give me this water that I
> may not thirst, nor come here to draw" (4:15).

> I know the Messiah is coming (he who is called Christ);
> when he comes he will show us all things (4:25).

> So the woman left her water jug and went away into
> the city and said to the people, "Come see a man who
> told me all that I ever did. Can this be the Christ?"
> (4:28–29).

Commentators do not agree on the historicity of the narrative. Like the previous study of Nicodemus, the narrative was probably composed by the evangelist with some historical foundation. Many aspects of the chapter show points of contact with Old Testament themes as well as rabbinic tradition. Whatever the origin of the narrative, the author focuses on the encounter between Jesus and the woman.

A study of the development of the themes involved highlights the relationship between Jesus and the woman:

verses 7–10: the first exchange introduces the topic of living water and challenges the woman.
verses 11–15: the woman misunderstands and Jesus clarifies that he is speaking of the water of eternal life to which the woman responds by requesting this water. Still, the woman has yet to recognize Jesus.
verses 16–18: Jesus takes the initiative by speaking of her personal life, leading her to recognize who he is.
verses 19–26: the woman recognizes that Jesus is a prophet and

turns the conversation away from her personal life to ask about worship. Jesus explains that true worship can come only from those begotten by the Spirit. Finally, the woman recognizes Jesus as the messiah and affirms her conclusion by becoming a missionary to her townsfolk.

The episode narrates a gradual unfolding of the self-revelation of Jesus, with many of the Johannine themes involved: revelation, the need for a personal decision of faith, the influence of the power of God, messianic titles, all on various levels of meaning. The conclusion of the episode includes the reaction of the townspeople as well: they too come to faith not on the word of the woman but through their own experience of Jesus.

> They said to the woman, "It is no longer because of your words that we believe, for we have heard for ourselves, and now know that this is indeed the Savior of the world" (4:42).

The chapter also presents the familiar christological theme of the author that unites the revelation of Jesus to the faith of the individual. The use of "I am," the title "messiah," and the implications of "Father"—all point to the fundamental christology of this gospel. Jesus reveals God to those who are receptive.

The Samaritan woman has serious personal problems. She may have gone to the well at midday to avoid meeting other women of the town. She was a Samaritan, and so despised by the Jews. She was a woman, and so on a lower level of society than men. She was probably notorious in the town because of her five husbands. Yet, she was bold and open to Jesus. On his part, Jesus never condemned her but gradually led her to faith. She responded and became a changed person.

The Samaritan woman exemplifies the active receptivity needed in one who will follow Jesus. Jesus does not call just the righteous but anyone who is open to his message. Once she has acknowledged Jesus in her life, she, like John the Baptist before her, fulfills her responsibility as a follower by leading others to Jesus. Her lack of understanding, her background, need not prevent her from acceptance, and her continual bold probing and prodding lead her to full faith.

■ The Royal Official ■

Please read John 4:46–53; Matthew 8:5–13; Luke 7:1–10.

Some contemporary commentators assign this encounter between Jesus and the royal official to pre-Johannine material. The story in this gospel agrees in many details with the cures described in Matthew 8:5–13 and Luke 7:1–10. All three narrate the same event, even though the approaches differ considerably.

This author indicates the function of the official in verse 50: "The man put his trust in the word Jesus spoke to him, and started for home." As the faith of the centurion of Matthew and Luke occasioned the cure of the son, so the faith of the royal official in the word of Jesus occasioned the miracle narrated here. The Johannine narrative, however, is not as explicit about the faith of the official as is Matthew. Further differences become evident as the comparison continues. According to the Fourth Gospel the word the Johannine Jesus speaks gives life. The word of Jesus in the Fourth Gospel does not simply heal. The royal official believed in the word of the Lord, which brought life. The faith results from coming to Jesus in a receptive way, listening to his word and finally accepting this life-giving word. The Johannine Jesus speaks and makes people alive.

The royal official in this gospel represents all those who listen to the Word of God believing and trusting that this one Word will not only heal them but give them life. The Word of God expressed in Jesus continues through the preaching of the followers of Jesus and through the word of scripture. As the royal official listened to the Word, so members of the Johannine community listened to the Word and accepted the Word. They experienced eternal life. The Word had become flesh in Jesus, and those who hear the Word and respond join Jesus with God—and God gives them eternal life as he has given eternal life to Jesus.

■ The Lame Man and the Man Born Blind ■

Please read John 5:1–18; 9:1–41.

The stories of the lame man in chapter 5 and the man born blind in chapter 9 have a similar structure. Each begins with a miracle, and each leads to a controversy between Jesus and the Jews. The author loosely links the controversy to the miracle story by mentioning that it occurred on the Sabbath. Both narratives also reflect the controversy between church and synagogue at the time of the gospel rather than the actual ministry of Jesus.

The lame man does not at first know Jesus' identity (5:13). Thus Jesus seeks him out a second time, offering a second opportunity for faith after his cure. The cured man has experienced the healing power of Jesus and then faced a moment critical for faith. Unfortunately, he remains content with the cure and does not come to faith. Jesus offered the opportunity, but the man ignored it. The lame man preferred to remain on the level of the physical and failed to rise to the spiritual level. The divinity of Jesus shines through the humanity, the spiritual through the physical, but not all can see it.

The blind man, on the contrary, exemplifies an occasion when the sign, the miracle, led to faith. The author constructs his narrative to emphasize the hardening of the nonbelieving Jews in the presence of the revelation of Jesus and the gradual unfolding of faith on the part of the receptive blind man.

First he confesses that Jesus is a prophet ("What do you say about him since he has opened your eyes?" He said, "He is a prophet" [9:17]). Then he sees Jesus as a man from God ("If this man were not from God he could do nothing" [9:33]). Finally he believes in him as the Son of Man ("Do you believe in the Son of man?"…He said, "Lord I believe" [9:35, 38]). The sick, sinful man becomes the healthy, good man who sees. Those who appear to see, who appear to be good and healthy, are revealed as bad, unhealthy and blind.

The story contains some of the chief theological themes of the gospel. Jesus does the works of his Father (9:4). Jesus is the light, and he offers this light to people so that they may see (9:5). In the final section Jesus reveals himself as the Son of Man (9:35). Within the dialogue the blind man calls Jesus a prophet (9:17) and a man from God (9:33). An oblique reference to Jesus as messiah occurs in the explanation of the fear of the parents (9:22).

Jesus manifests himself and gradually the blind man "sees" and believes. Unlike the lame man, the blind man does not stop at the cure, the physical level, but moves to the spiritual level. He believes in Jesus as the Son of Man, the prophet sent from God. The author contrasts the profession of personal acceptance of Jesus by the blind man with the Pharisees' refusal to accept Jesus. God directs the revelation of Jesus to the individual, inviting a positive response. The free offer expects a free response. The one least likely to respond accepts in faith the revelation of God. Those in the better position to respond, the Pharisees, not only reject Jesus but refuse to acknowledge the miracle Jesus performed.

The lame man and the blind man represent others within both the Johannine context and the context of Christianity. Experiencing good things does not of necessity lead to belief in God or in Jesus. Some people can see the hand of God everywhere. Others can never believe in the hand of God. Some freely accept and believe; others go their merry way never coming to faith, even when surrounded by signs of God's goodness and love.

■ Philip ■

Please read John 1:43–51; 6:1–15; 12:20–36; 14:1–14.

Philip in the Fourth Gospel seems rather complex. He appears in four places: 1:43–51; 6:1–15; 12:20–36; 14:1–14. That in itself is unusual. He appears once in Mark and Matthew and twice in Luke. The interpretation of the last three appearances in this gospel depends on the remembrance of Philip in the opening chapter: as a believing disciple. He heard the call and accepted Jesus as "the one of whom Moses in the law and also the prophets wrote" (1:45). In this episode, however, Nathanael overshadows Philip. He comes into his own only when the other places in which he appears are united and compared.

Philip in chapter 6 seems to be a believer who does not understand. Jesus, aware of the misunderstanding, gives further guidance. Philip finds it hard to believe that anyone can feed such a large multitude but learns from the experience that Jesus has such power.

The third occurrence (12:20–36) also presents Philip as the misunderstanding disciple. He had made his commitment to Jesus, but he did not fully appreciate the manner in which God was present in Jesus. He wanted a manifestation of God, a theophany such as Moses or the elders of Israel had experienced. But no such theophany would by given to Philip. Jesus revealed God in a human way, expressed in the ordinary aspects of human life. Jesus revealed the human face of God. The follower who looked at Jesus could see God.

The final appearance of Philip casts this disciple in yet another role. In chapter 12 the Greeks wish to see Jesus and ask Philip, who speaks to Andrew. Both disciples bear Greek names. Previously Philip was identified as coming from Galilee, the land of the gentiles in a Jewish tradition. The symbolism seems complete. Just as the Samaritan woman introduced her fellow Samaritans to Jesus, so the Greeks are introduced to Jesus by Philip, who represents the Greek disciples. He also was a missionary and could never be hindered from his acceptance of the Lord in spite of his lack of full understanding.

Philip represents the misunderstanding disciple who yet remains faithful. He has many questions and wants things his own way, but he never fails in his fundamental acceptance of faith in Jesus. He also represents those who act as missionaries to their own people. Once a person has accepted Jesus, the expected outcome directs the believers to invite those within their own community and family to follow Jesus as well. Knowing God in Jesus impels the believer to reach out to others so that they too may have the opportunity to see God in Jesus.

■ Martha, Mary and Lazarus ■

Please read John 11:1–44; 12:1–8.

Throughout the narrative of the raising of Lazarus, Martha believes in Jesus, but her faith needs further development. She addresses Jesus with lofty titles probably used in the early profession of faith by believers: Lord, Christ, the Son of God, he who is coming into the world (11:27). She does not, however, yet believe that he has power to give life. She sees Jesus as a divine intermediary between God and people (11:22) but not as the giver of life (11:25). Jesus aids her faith by showing the deeper truth behind the lofty titles. He acts out a drama of the gift of life by raising Lazarus, which proves to Martha that he has power to give life in the present and not just in the future. Jesus does not reject her traditional understanding of faith or the titles she chose to use, but he sought to demonstrate the deeper truth behind the titles. Martha found it difficult to believe that Jesus brings life into this present world. Jesus offers a dramatic assurance by calling her brother to life. Martha came to understand that the word of Jesus gives life now as well as in the future.

Mary meets Jesus in this same chapter and falls at his feet. But like her sister, she does not demonstrate a particularly deep faith. She too used the right words but without complete understanding. Mary will also come to believe that Jesus is the messiah who will give life to all who believe in him. Jesus will demonstrate further the result of personal faith when he speaks his word and Lazarus comes out of the tomb. Jesus raised Lazarus to attest to the future resurrection for all of those who believe in him *now*. Jesus comes into this world as messiah (11:27), the Son of God who gives life to all who hear his word and believe in him. Eternal life belongs in the present as well as in the future.

Like other individuals, Martha, Mary and Lazarus offer insights into the development of faith. Lofty titles mean nothing unless they lead an individual to trust. Martha and Mary ultimately trust in Jesus, and Jesus responds by raising Lazarus, who comes alive when hearing the word of Jesus. Jesus can save all from eternal death not just in the future but *now*. The word of Jesus gives life. Misunderstanding gives way to a sure belief that the present life has already experienced the beginning of eternal life.

The two sisters and Lazarus appear again in the following chapter, in which Jesus joins them at dinner. Martha served and Mary anointed the feet of Jesus. This scene joins together two traditions from the synoptics: Mark 14:3–9 and Luke 10:38–41. The author of the Fourth Gospel joins the story of Martha and Mary—with one doing the work and the other enjoying the company of Jesus—to another story of the anointing of his feet. Friends of Jesus enjoy his company. They also respond to his needs by caring for him physically and even performing this ordinary sign of Eastern hospitality. Unknown to Mary, she anoints Jesus for his burial. True followers do what is necessary to make Jesus feel welcome. Many times they are not fully aware of the consequences of their actions, yet they respond because they believe.

■ Judas ■

Please read John 6:67–71; 12:1–8; 13:2, 26–30; 18:2–5.

No presentation of the followers of Jesus could neglect Judas. He appears as one of the twelve (6:67–71); at the anointing of Jesus (12:1–8); in the supper scene (13:2, 26–30) and in the passion account (18:2–5). Each scene has a parallel in the synoptic tradition, but in this gospel the author adds his own understanding of this onetime follower. The evangelist borrowed from the general traditions about Judas. He was a betrayer but also a thief (12:6); he takes what is not his own. He is a figure of darkness (13:30). Once he came to the light but decided to return to the darkness. The devil has entered him ("And during the Supper, when the devil had already put it into the heart of Judas Iscariot, Simon's son, to betray him" [13:2].) and as a result he allied himself with the enemies of the Lord.

Judas exemplifies the person to whom faith was offered and rejected. He could have walked in the light but chose the darkness.

> So after receiving the morsel, he immediately went out;
> and it was night (13:30).

At the moment of the passion two worlds stand in conflict: the world of God the Father and Jesus and faith and light, and the world of the devil and evil and darkness. Jesus represented one world, Judas the other.

In the opening scene of the passion Jesus asked the question, "Who is it you want?" (18:4). This is the ultimate question about Jesus in the Fourth Gospel. The crowds, with Judas, answered, "Jesus of Nazareth" (18:5). Jesus then responded "I am" *(ego eimi)* (18:5, 6, 8). The expression evokes awe and adoration. The formula reveals Jesus, the presence of God, to those who come to the light and believe. Judas stands by and does nothing. He had been present in the ministry of Jesus. He should have recognized the presence of the divine in Jesus. Jesus called him to faith. He could walk always in the light, but Judas chose the darkness and turned away from Jesus, the one true light. In the confrontation between the world of light and darkness, Jesus confronted Judas, but he moved into the darkness and refused to believe.

■   Mary, the Mother of Jesus   ■

Please read John 2:1–11; 6:42; 19:25–27.

Any study of individuals in the gospel must include the mother of Jesus. Mary appears in only two episodes in this gospel (Cana 2:1–11 and Calvary 19:25–27) and is called not by her name but only the mother of Jesus. The crowds make mention of her in John 6:42 when they are divided about the meaning of the activity of Jesus and remark: "Is this not Jesus, the son of Joseph? Do we not know his father and mother?" In the gospel Mary makes no profession of faith, and when Jesus speaks to her, he uses the title "woman." Mary says few words: "They have no wine" (2:3) and "Do whatever he tells you" (2:5).

From earliest times the figure of the mother of Jesus in this gospel has been interpreted symbolically. She is the new Eve, the symbol of the church, or of Jewish Christianity, but more than any other symbolism she exemplifies a complete and total faith in Jesus. She believes in him, and with that firm trust awaits the fulfillment of her faith. Mary remains steadfast in her commitment. She did not need to have her faith explained, nor does the author offer any reference to the genesis of her faith. At Cana she believed that Jesus would never allow the wedding couple to be embarrassed. She believed that Jesus would respond to their need. She did not seem to understand the meaning of the "hour," but that did not prevent her from appealing to her Son. At Calvary she joined the Beloved Disciple in a common faith and a common expectation of the full revelation that would take place at the "hour" of Jesus, his glorification. Mary demonstrates both the need for fidelity and its reward.

Mary in this gospel does not represent a person coming to faith but rather one who has already believed and who remains steadfast in faith in spite of a lack of full understanding. Mary needs no explanation for her faith. Mary is the perfect and ideal believer. Mary demonstrates the need for fidelity and the reward for fidelity when no full explanation can ever be possible. The author never uses her proper name, for the mother of Jesus transcends any one proper name. She is mother not only of Jesus but of all believers. She is woman, for she fulfills a human destiny as a woman of faith.

■ Mary Magdalene ■

Please read John 20:1–2, 11–18.

Mary Magdalene appears in two passages in the same chapter (20:1–2, 11–18). The latter is a dramatic presentation of her faith response to the risen Lord. The former refers to her visit to the empty tomb, similar to the visit to the tomb in the synoptics. Here the evangelist singles out Mary Magdalene and in so doing de-emphasizes the events of Easter morning in order to emphasize Calvary. Not women but only Mary Magdalene goes to the tomb on that Easter morning.

> Jesus said to her, "Woman why are you weeping? Whom do you seek?" Supposing him to be the gardener, she said to him, "Sir, if you have carried him away, tell me where you have laid him, and I will take him away." Jesus said to her, "Mary." She turned and said to him in Hebrew "Rabboni" (which means Teacher) (20:15–16).

Some see the encounter between Mary and Jesus as having an apologetic undertone. The objection that the disciples have stolen the body of the Lord cannot be valid since the possibility of grave robbing is raised by one of the followers of Jesus. The main purpose of the evangelist, however, seems to be the presentation of faith in the risen Lord and not any apologetic. Jesus called Mary by name, just as the Good Shepherd calls his sheep by name (10:3). She responded by calling him Rabbi (teacher) as did the first two disciples and Nicodemus (1:38; 3:2). Mary at first does not understand the meaning of the resurrection and wishes to cling to him (20:17). Jesus himself interprets its meaning. The risen Lord must ascend to the Father. Jesus did not return to life through resuscitation; he is risen. After Mary realized the meaning of the resurrection she announced: "I have seen the Lord" (20:18). Mary had to become an evangelist to announce his resurrection to others. Mary heralds this proclamation of faith. The gospel uses the example of Mary to enhance the depth of faith expected of an individual. Before, Jesus was accepted as one who revealed God the Father; now, after his resurrection, Jesus must be believed as the one who has returned to the Father and who will bring all to the same God the Father giving eternal life to all who believe.

■ Thomas ■

Please read John 11:16; 14:5; 20:24–29.

Thomas appears in this gospel as one of the disciples in 11:16 and in this episode joins the resurrection of Lazarus to the approaching death of Jesus. Thomas is willing to die with Jesus. In 14:5 he is the unknowing disciple: "Lord, we do not know where you are going; how can we know the way?" Even before he appears in the twentieth chapter, Thomas is the disciple with bravado who will die with Jesus and the disciple who just does not understand.

In chapter 20 Thomas finally overcomes his doubt about the resurrection and believes in Jesus because he has experienced him. He doubted the testimony of the other disciples who had seen the Lord. He wanted to put his fingers into the wounds of the nails and his hand in the wound of the lance. Jesus appears and Thomas explicitly makes a profession of faith in the divinity of Jesus: "My Lord and my God" (20:28). The final verse discloses the situation of all later communities: individuals must believe in the risen Lord as Thomas did, but without the actual appearance of Jesus: "Blessed are those who have not seen and yet believe" (20:29).

In some ways the doubting Thomas is incidental to the main point of this narrative. The reality of the resurrection and Thomas's belief in Jesus as risen form the central meaning of the episode.

They set the stage for the profession of faith in verse 28. Thomas explicitly professes belief in the divinity of Jesus, the crucified One who is risen. Jesus is for Thomas "both Lord and God," which is the profession of faith of every follower of Jesus. Jesus has become both Lord and God for people, Jesus crucified and risen.

The final saying by Jesus may also reflect the situation of the community of John: individuals who believe as Thomas did but without the appearance of the risen Lord. Even the profession of faith by Thomas may come from the attempt of the later Christian community to join together a belief in the humanity and divinity of Jesus. Thomas has his problems. Jesus however is present to him and the doubts and problems vanish. The true believer never allows doubts to destroy his or her fundamental commitment. Jesus still reveals God.

■   Peter   ■

Please read John 1:41; 6:8, 68; 13:6, 9, 24, 36; 18:10, 15, 25; 20:2, 4, 6; 21:2–25.

Peter figures prominently in all four gospels. In the Fourth Gospel he appears frequently (see the passages listed above). These passages have some similarity to the synoptic tradition but also present a peculiar Johannine nuance. Often Peter functions in a subordinate position to the Beloved Disciple. Jesus changes the name of Simon in chapter 1, after he has been led to Jesus through Andrew his brother. In chapter 6 he speaks for the twelve in his profession of faith:

> "You have the words of eternal life and we have believed
> and we have come to know that you are the holy one of
> God" (6:68–69).

The synoptic tradition also presented Peter as confessing belief in the messiahship of Jesus. The Fourth Gospel bases this messiahship, however, on the presupposition that Jesus reveals God. To be messiah in the Fourth Gospel does not mean the same thing as the messiah meant in the Old Testament tradition.

Peter also appears at the Last Supper, again in a subordinate position to the Beloved Disciple (13:6, 9, 24, 36). He does not want Jesus to wash his feet, but when faced with the prospect of having no part of the inheritance of Jesus, he typically goes too far and wants Jesus to wash his hands and head as well (13:6–9). The Beloved Disciple takes no part in the foot washing, but later Peter turns to him and asks him to intervene with the Lord regarding the identity of the betrayer. It seems that only the Beloved Disciple learned the identity of the one who would betray Jesus (13:24–26).

The scene at the empty tomb (20:3–10) also offers a contrast. The Beloved Disciple arrived at the tomb first but waited for Peter, who looked in and saw that the tomb was empty but did not believe. The Beloved Disciple looked in "and he saw and believed" (20:8). Peter did not come to faith in the risen Lord because of the empty tomb but only through an experience of Jesus as risen. The Beloved Disciple saw and believed.

In the final chapter Peter is listed first among the disciples (21:2), described as a fisherman (21:3, 11) and one to whom the risen Lord has revealed himself (21:14). The focus of the chapter centers on the pastoral office of Peter.

> Jesus said to Simon Peter, "Simon, son of John, do you love me more than these?" He said to him, "Yes, Lord, you know that I love you." He said to him, "Feed my lambs." A second time he said to him, "Simon, son of John, do you love me?" He said to him, "Yes, Lord; you know that I love you." He said to him, "Tend my sheep." He said to him the third time, "Simon, son of John, do you love me?" Peter was grieved because he said to him the third time, "Do you love me?" And he said to him, "Lord, you know everything; you know that I love you." Jesus said to him, "Feed my sheep" (20:15–17).

Peter had come to faith in the risen Lord; once he has professed his love of Jesus, then he can lead the sheep. Peter had passed his test of love in this chapter, after he had previously failed the test of fidelity in the passion of Jesus. Once he has professed both faith and love he can assume his responsibility as the leader of the disciples. Earlier Peter had believed in the revealer and spoke for the disciples. Now he assumes a close relationship with Jesus through personal choice and commitment and accepts the care of the sheep.

The one who believes in Jesus must love the brethren. This is true for all followers but especially for those in leadership positions. Failure, sin and infidelity do not condemn a believer forever. Repentance is always possible. The Lord does not hold grudges but willingly forgives any follower. Peter reminds all to be careful of faith and especially of love. If a disciple fails, Jesus asks only that he or she again believe and love.

■ The Beloved Disciple ■

Please read John 13:2–26; 18:15–16; 19:25–27; 20:2–10; 21:2–24.

The Beloved Disciple appears with Peter in the final chapter (21:2–7; 19–24), at the Last Supper (13:2–26), at the foot of the cross (19:25–27) and in the race to the tomb (20:2–10). In the latter he is also called "the other disciple"; for this reason he is usually identified with "the other disciple" in chapter 18:15–16 during the passion. The Beloved Disciple is not just another believer among many but epitomizes the believer, the disciple, the beloved, the one who gives witness.

As believer, the Beloved Disciple contrasts with Peter at the tomb. Neither Mary Magdalene nor Peter come to faith in the risen Lord at the tomb. For the man who represents the believer par excellence, the empty tomb is sufficient. He has not seen but he has believed.

In the final chapter the Beloved Disciple proclaims to Peter: "It is the Lord" (21:7). He recognizes him immediately. He is the disciple. He followed Jesus and believed in his word. In the gospel of John discipleship extends beyond the group known as the twelve, and so the Beloved Disciple need not be identified with one of the twelve. He probably became a follower of the Lord only in Jerusalem, which would explain why he was known to the group surrounding the high priest (18:15–16). He followed from the Last Supper to the courtyard of the high priest to Calvary.

This disciple is also described as the one whom Jesus loved (13:23; 19:26; 20:2; 21:7, 20) and preeminently deserves to be called a friend of Jesus (15:15). At the Last Supper he reclined on the breast of Jesus (13:25) and shared a community of faith with Mary, the mother of the Lord (19:26–27).

Because of his relationship with Jesus he could give witness and testimony. His faith and love qualified the Beloved Disciple to lead others to believe and to have eternal life. He had witnessed:

> He who saw this has borne witness and his testimony is true and he knows that he tells the truth that you also may believe (19:35).

In the final chapter the author makes reference to the testimony of the Beloved Disciple continuing in the church through his account of the life and death and resurrection of Jesus, the Johannine gospel. The testimony remains.

The Beloved Disciple exemplifies all that faith in Jesus implies. He shows the fidelity of Mary, the acceptance of Nathanael, of Peter, of Mary Magdalene. He never doubts, never misunderstands, but always knows in whom he has placed his trust. He then bears testimony and invites others to follow Jesus as well.

This analysis of disciples could continue. The divine and human Jesus fulfills his mission only when people come to believe in him. Each follower can offer some appreciation of faith, but it is the Mother of Jesus and the Beloved Disciple who best manifest the ideal believers. These individuals personify the fundamental need for a personal commitment to the Lord. With this faith comes the possibility of the love that alone binds individuals to Jesus and to each other.

Suggestions for Reflection

1. The study of individuals in the gospel can be fascinating. How have you been affected by the various characters? Do you relate to some more than to others?

2. Compare Nicodemus and the Samaritan woman. Examine in particular their personalities as portrayed in the gospel. How would you relate to them as individuals?

3. Mary is a firm believer. From your appreciation of Mary, the mother of Jesus, compare her with the image in popular piety. What makes her so attractive in this gospel?

4. The Beloved Disciple is the ideal believer. Do you think of him as a historical figure or not?

5. Pick one of the other individuals or several of them and compare them with Mary and the Beloved Disciple. How can the presence of so many people advance the meaning of faith in Jesus?

6. Faith is primary in this gospel. How can the study of individuals help in understanding faith? What is involved in faith in Jesus? How much commitment is really required?

7. The christology of this gospel includes the acceptance in faith. How does this affect the teaching about Jesus in the church?

3.

Faith and Love:
The Foundations of the Community

*T*he gospel of John seems to have two endings, one in chapter 20 and one in chapter 21.

> Jesus performed many other signs as well, signs not recorded here, in the presence of his disciples. But these have been recorded to help you believe that Jesus is the Messiah, the Son of God, so that through this faith you may have life in his name (20:30–31).

> It is this same disciple who is the witness to these things: it is he who wrote them down and his testimony, we know is true. There are still many other things Jesus did, yet if they were written down, I doubt there would be room enough in the entire world to hold the books to record them (21:24–25).

The first ending reflects either a missionary purpose, an attempt to enkindle faith in those who do not yet believe, or a homiletic purpose, to strengthen and confirm the faith of an already constituted congregation. The second ending can be interpreted as directed to the congregation or perhaps to other Christian congregations as an apologetic to defend the contents of the gospel. The first ending also emphasizes the importance of faith to the author and inspirer of the gospel. The second ending attempts to authenticate the particular approach in the gospel itself by referring to the source of the tradition as well as remarking that no book could ever contain all that Jesus said and did. The Jesus tradition goes beyond all efforts to record it.

■ Faith in the Fourth Gospel ■

Faith in the Fourth Gospel is the human response to the revelation of Jesus. This faith consists in an active acceptance, seen in
the author's choice of a verb *to believe* rather than just the noun
belief. Jesus demands a decision as he encounters individuals. The
individual becomes aware of need and the reality of sin and darkness. When Jesus enters into an individual's life, the person loses
all false illusions and accepts the salvation offered. The believer
accepts Jesus not just as a miracle worker but as the Son of God.
Once accepted personally, the words of Jesus become revelatory and
lead to the acceptance by God the Father.

■ Faith and God the Father ■

God the Father plays a significant role in the birth of faith.
The Father gives the disciples to Jesus; the Father then draws
the disciples to faith in Jesus and actually teaches them through
the words of Jesus. Faith in this gospel becomes a gift of God the
Father:

> All that the Father gives me shall come to me; and him
> who comes to me I shall not cast out (6:37).

> No one can come to me unless the Father who sent me
> draws him (6:44).

The author writes of the close relationship between Jesus and
God. The Father has sent Jesus into the world. The evangelist
knows also the need for a divine initiative if the individual is to
recognize the presence of God the Father through Jesus and his
preaching:

> Philip said to him, "Lord show us the Father and we shall
> be satisfied." Jesus said to him, "Have I been with you so
> long, and yet you do not know me, Philip? He who has
> seen me has seen the Father" (14:8–9).

> He who believes in me, believes not in me but in him who
> sent me. And he who sees me sees him who sent me
> (12:44–45).

God the Father speaks to the heart of the person, which enables the
individual to accept Jesus as the personal revelation of God. Jesus

reveals God humanly, and those who look on the face of Jesus, observe his works and listen to his words have found God. Jesus is God's human face.

■ Believing and Knowing ■

The relationship between Jesus and God the Father in the origin of a person's faith and in the content of that faith becomes especially evident in a studying the words *believing* and *knowing* in this gospel. They appear nearly two hundred times. Often the author used figurative references, which at times say more and other times say less than the words *to believe* or *to know*. Coming to light is a figurative expression of faith in Jesus; hearing the voice of the Good Shepherd and recognizing it figuratively expresses coming to faith within a parable. Remaining close to the vine in the parable of the vine and the branches also expresses the relationship of faith. Believing and knowing—coming to Jesus and staying with him—are personal activities that pervade the entire gospel.

■ Individuals and Faith ■

The examination of the major and minor personages in the gospel shows that some believe and others do not; some know him and others fail to recognize him. His disciples appear under every possible heading, fluctuating, changing and making faltering advances as they come to believe and to know Jesus as God's personal envoy and their personal Lord and Savior. Eventually they acknowledge, like Thomas (20:28) that Jesus is both Lord and God for them.

The opening chapter of the gospel presents the image of light coming into a dark world, calling people to faith:

> In him was life and the life was the light of men. The light shines in the darkness and the darkness has not overcome it (1:4–5).

> But to all who received him, who believed in his name, he gave power to become children of God (1:12).

This same chapter narrates the call of the first disciples. In each instance, immediately, they made a profession of faith. Andrew told his brother Peter: "We have found the Messiah" (1:41). Philip told

Nathanael: "We have found him of whom Moses in the Law and also the prophets wrote" (1:45). Nathanael declared: "Rabbi, you are the Son of God, you are the king of Israel" (1:49). This opening chapter also situates the role of John the Baptist. He simply bears testimony to Jesus as the lamb of God and encourages his own disciples to follow Jesus (1:29–34). Each one encounters Jesus for the first time, and immediately they become believers and followers. Unlike the synoptic gospels, in which the apostles and disciples gradually come to faith, in this gospel the early followers seem to have full faith at the outset. By the end of the first chapter Jesus has followers who have full faith, for they have come to see God in Jesus. The chapter ends with a reference to Genesis 28:12. Just as Jacob recognized Bethel as a place to encounter God, so Jesus proclaims that on him, the Son of Man, the angels of God will ascend and descend (1:51).

Nicodemus comes from the darkness troubled by Jesus. He knows Jesus represents more than just a miracle worker: "No one can do these signs that you do unless God is with him" (3:2). But, as already seen, Nicodemus does not make his profession of faith and probably never does. His interest and concern for Jesus easily could be contrasted with the Samaritan woman, who is receptive to Jesus and ultimately not only makes her profession of faith but also becomes an evangelist, inviting her townspeople to listen to Jesus.

Judas, of course, received every opportunity to believe, to come to the light, but he preferred the darkness. At the Last Supper he left the upper room. The evangelist writes: "And it was night" (13:30). Jesus will not force anyone to believe in him. Faith is God's gift; it must be accepted in personal freedom.

> Jesus said to the twelve. "Will you also go away?" Simon Peter answered him. "Lord to whom shall we go? You have the words of eternal life" (6:67–68).

If Jesus allows those closest to him to go away, he also allows anyone to go away. Jesus never imposes. Jesus freely offers faith, and the individual freely responds.

The Jews, the leaders of the people, also had their opportunity to believe. Jesus taught daily in the temple. When questioned by the high priest, Jesus responded:

> "I have spoken openly to the world; I have always taught in synagogues and in the temple, where all Jews come together. I have said nothing secretly" (18:20).

But for many in this group, faith in Jesus became impossible. They could not recognize the presence of the God of Abraham, Isaac and Jacob in Jesus and ultimately denied their heritage at the trial of Jesus. When Pilate asked the Jews, "Shall I crucify your king?" the leaders answered, "We have no king but Caesar" (19:15). In the history of Israel God alone was their true king, and even when they had an earthly king, his presence represented their true king, God. The Jews in the passion of the Lord not only fail to come to faith in Jesus but actually reject their own faith as expressed in the Old Testament traditions.

■ The Content of Faith ■

The actual content of faith and knowing becomes evident in almost every chapter: Jesus and his mission. The object of knowing, however, is different in this gospel from the object of believing. When the author uses the word *to know,* he rarely uses simple nouns or pronouns. These are common, however, with the use of the word to *believe. To believe in,* with an accusative, in two instances has God as the object: "He who believes in me believes not in me but in him who sent me" (12:44); and "Let not your hearts be troubled; believe in God, believe also in me" (14:1). In all other instances individuals are asked to believe in Jesus,

When the author uses the verb *to believe* with a dative, the objects are transitional. They are testimonies, words of Jesus or signs. In each case the sign points to the meaning of the mission of Jesus:

> They believed the scripture and the word Jesus had spoken (2:22).

> "Even though you do not believe me, believe the works that you may know and understand that the Father is in me and I am in the Father" (10:38).

The results of believing and knowing Jesus are eternal life or the entering into eternal life:

> And this is eternal life that they know you the only true God and Jesus Christ whom you have sent (17:3).

> Whoever believes in him should not perish but have eternal life (3:16).

The individual believes in Jesus and his mission, comes to know him and who he is, and understands what God has sent Jesus to accomplish. Then the individual believes and possesses eternal life.

The author of this gospel stresses the relationship between believer and Jesus; he writes about the growth of faith, the role of God the Father in bringing people to faith and the content of that faith: Jesus and his mission. The established purpose of the gospel helps individuals "to believe that Jesus is the Christ, the Son of God and that believing you may have life in his name" (20:31). If no faith exists, then for the community of this gospel, no Christian community could possibly exist. When the ending in chapter 20 is compared to the ending of chapter 21, in all probability the original readers of the gospel recognized the effort on the part of the final editor to justify this emphasis on the necessity of faith as the foundation of the Christian community. The essential need for this faith relationship is particularly expressed in the parable of the Good Shepherd.

■ The Shepherd ■

Please read John 10:1–18.

The image of the shepherd and the flock appears frequently in Near Eastern literature. In the Old Testament the book of Numbers used the image of shepherd when Moses asked God for someone to share in his authority (Nm 27:17). Zechariah used a similar image (Zec 11:4), and the prophet Ezekiel used the image of the shepherd not only for the leaders of Israel but also for God (Ez 34).

Each of the synoptics used the same image. Mark presented Jesus as the shepherd: "I will strike the shepherd and the sheep shall be scattered: (Mk 14:27). Matthew recorded the parable of the lost sheep (Mt 18:12–14). Finally, Luke used the image in two places: he referred to the disciples as a flock: "Fear not little flock, for it is your Father's good pleasure to give you the kingdom" (12:32); and he also recorded the parable of the Lost Sheep (Lk 15:3–7).

What characterizes the parable of the Good Shepherd in the gospel of John is the reciprocal relationship between Jesus and the individual sheep. The sheepfold is unified by Jesus alone. Jesus has a close and intimate relationship with each sheep, grounded on the union and relationship between Jesus and his Father. The chapter actually contains two intertwined parables: the Shepherd and the

Sheep, and the Door and the Sheepfold. In each the author presents the parable and then explains its meaning:

> The sheep hear his voice as he calls his own by name and leads them out. When he has brought out (all) those that are his, he walks in front of them, and the sheep follow him because they recognize his voice. They will not follow a stranger; such a one they will flee, because they do not recognize a stranger's voice (10:3b-5).

This parable finds its explanation after the author has explained the meaning of the Door and the Sheepfold:

> I am the good shepherd; the good shepherd lays down his life for the sheep. The hired hand, who is no shepherd nor owner of the sheep, catches sight of the wolf coming and runs away, leaving the sheep to be scattered by the wolf. That is because he works for pay; he has no concern for the sheep. I am the good shepherd. I know my sheep and my sheep know me in the same way that the Father knows me and I know the Father; for these sheep I will give my life. I have other sheep that do not belong to this fold. I must lead them too, and they shall hear my voice. So there shall be one flock, one shepherd (10:11–16).

In the presentation of the parable (10:3b–5) Jesus calls his sheep by name. They know his voice. He does not confuse them with anyone else, and they feel secure when they hear the familiar sound of his voice. Calling by name has a long biblical tradition implying intimacy as well as power and influence. Jesus knows his sheep sufficiently well to call them personally by name. He unites the individual with himself, and the individual feels secure in following the Lord.

The Parable Interpreted

In the interpretation of the parable (10:11–16) the author again expresses the intimate knowledge between shepherd and sheep. The Old Testament knew of the intimate knowledge that existed between God and the chosen people: "He knows those who take refuge in him" (Na 1:7). Jesus exemplifies this intimate knowledge, for through him God expressed care for the flock. The mission of Jesus in this parable makes clear the intimacy that also exists between Jesus and his Father. Jesus came from God and is for God; Jesus is nothing apart from what he is for God. Thus Jesus could reveal God. The full parable also brings out God being for Jesus and his followers. Because Jesus is united with his sheep, then God is also for the followers of the Lord.

Once a believer has heard the voice of the Good Shepherd and has followed, he or she can feel secure. Jesus as God's revealer promises nourishment and protection and a loving intimacy. Jesus knows the names of his followers. They hear his voice and follow.

Unity

Verse 16 stresses the purpose of this knowledge: to bring all to unity. A mutual knowledge exists between Jesus and God, and Jesus and the flock. This mutual knowledge unites the flock to God. For the author of this gospel, this union of God and his envoy, Jesus, and the believer makes eternal life possible for humankind. The sheep know the shepherd; the believer knows God the Father and the one sent by the Father. Thus the believer has eternal life: "And this is eternal life, that they know the only true God and Jesus Christ whom you have sent" (17:3). This verse explains eternal life differently from the way most Christians are accustomed to believe. Eternal life is *now;* it is given to all who know the God whom Jesus has revealed.

The unity that exists between Father and Son is also expressed by the Son being in the Father and the Father being in the Son (10:38; 14:11; 17:21). The author also used the expression "the Son knows the Father" (10:15; 17:25). Jesus as the Good Shepherd who knows his sheep implies a relationship that is similar to that of Jesus and God his Father. As the Son knows the Father and receives life from him, so those who know the Son know the Father and receive eternal life. An eternal and stringent bond unites the individual believer with the Lord. They cannot be separated, for they are bound by faith. Once individuals respond in faith and become united with Jesus, the mutual bond of unity between God and Jesus carries them into the same unity. God has bound all believers together, and all are one with God.

The Meaning of the Flock

Historically, "the flock" has been interpreted in many different ways. It appears that some of the sheep in the sheepfold are not of the flock of Jesus; only those who hear his voice belong to him. The image of many flocks in one sheepfold, each belonging to a different shepherd, fits the conditions of the time. In the morning the different shepherds entered the fold, and the sheep who belonged to them followed them out to pasture. Such an interpretation of the parable could imply that the larger flock symbolized the Jews at the time of Jesus. Only some of them heard the voice and followed.

The reference to sheep belonging to other folds could further call to mind the gentiles and their call to faith in Jesus. Still further, the flock could be interpreted in a Gnostic sense. Late Judaism and early Christianity encountered a religious theory that emphasized knowledge bringing salvation to the world. An original unity in light had been broken and the light had been dispersed in each individual. A revealer would come to offer secret knowledge that would unite the separated sparks once again into a primordial light. As knowledge was the means by which the Gnostic redeemer united individuals and brought salvation, so some saw in this parable the mutual knowledge of Jesus and his flock that brings salvation and eternal life. Whatever value and influence Gnosticism may have had on Christianity, such a theory runs counter to the teaching of this gospel, for in the Fourth Gospel love and not knowledge, however important, brings salvation.

The Flock United in Faith

Whatever the interpretation, the collective aspect is evident, even if some do not belong to the group. The flock is diversified, with some united (those who hear his voice) with Jesus. Others remain separated (those who do not respond to his voice). The flock also seems open to growth (other sheep outside). In the interpretation of the parable Jesus remains the sole principle of unity based upon his unity with God the Father. The unity that exists among the sheep is only implicit. Since they have a personal relationship with the shepherd, they may also have personal relationships among themselves, but this dimension remains in the background. The author chose to stress in this parable the faith relationship between Jesus and the individual without discussing the relationship that also exists among believers.

The parable could mirror the historical situation of the call of Jesus to the Jews. It also may mirror the historical situation of the troubled Johannine community, separated from the synagogue, experiencing divisions within itself as well as problems in relating to other Christian communities. The parable would recognize the divisions but would also offer hope for a final unity, both within the community and without, in the future. When the final unity occurs, Jesus the Good Shepherd will be responsible, for he alone calls his flock.

The importance of a personal relationship, a faith commitment to Jesus by the individual person, remains paramount. This parable insists on the need to remain with Jesus as leader and guide and to continue to respond to his voice. At first glance the image of the shepherd and flock might appear to be an image of the church, but such a conclusion needs careful nuancing. The parable concerns a personal and individual relationship with Jesus. In that relationship, because of the image of a flock, any reference to a community is made only implicitly. For this gospel a community exists only because individual believers unite with Jesus in faith. The second parable in this gospel, the Vine and the Branches, completes the author's call for the essentials, for in this parable the faith that unites the individual with Jesus finds its expression in the love that binds believers together.

The Love of the Brethren

Please read John 15:1—16:4.
The synoptic gospels record many parables spoken by Jesus. In all likelihood Jesus used parables as his principal manner of teaching. If the Fourth Gospel contains only two parables, the Good Shepherd and the Vine and the Branches, this certainly manifests a specific choice by the author to single out the teachings of these parables as most important to the Jesus tradition. The first emphasizes faith, and the second emphasizes love.

■   The Twofold Commandment   ■

The synoptic gospels record the question put to Jesus by the inquiring scribe: "Which commandment is the first of all?" (Mk 12:28). Jesus responded with the well-known reply of the twofold commandment:

"The first is, 'Hear O Israel: The Lord our God the Lord is one; and you shall love the Lord your God with all your heart and with all your soul, and with all your mind, and with all your strength.' The second is this, 'You shall love your neighbor as yourself'" (Mk 12:29–31; see also Mt 22:34–40; Lk 10:25–28).

Jesus quotes from Deuteronomy 6:4, the reference to the first commandment, and then from Leviticus 19:18, the reference to the love of the neighbor. Each of the synoptics recorded this incident from the ministry of the Lord, and from this teaching, Christianity has developed its insistence on the close relationship between the love of God and the love of the neighbor.

Love of Enemies

Matthew and Luke also enjoin the followers of the Lord to love their enemies: "Love your enemies and pray for those who persecute you" (Mt 5:44); "Love your enemies, do good to those who hate you, bless those who persecute you, pray for those who abuse you" (Lk 6:27–28). Luke continues his call to expand the commandment of love by expecting the believers to turn the other cheek, to give cloak and coat to the one who takes, to give to all who beg and do to others as one would wish others to do oneself (Lk 6:29–31).

Christianity has flourished as a religion that offers love to all and will not discriminate even when the Christian faces rejection or persecution. The love of God and love of neighbor are irrevocably joined together. Matthew exemplifies this relationship when he records these words of Jesus:

> "So if you are offering your gift at the altar and there remember that your brother has something against you, leave your gift there before the altar and go first to be reconciled to your brother" (Mt 5:23–24).

■   The One Commandment in John   ■

How strange that the author of the Fourth Gospel fails to record this twofold commandment! This gospel emphasizes love but omits the two great commandments. It states that "the Father loves the Son" (5:20) and will love those who keep the commandments of the Lord, who respond to his word and together Jesus and his Father will come to those who love him (14:21–24). The author recounts the love of God for the Son and then completes the love relationship by including in that love all who come to believe in the Son. The mission of Jesus is to manifest the love of God for humankind: "For God so loved the world that he gave his only Son" (3:16). And the Father loves the Son precisely because the Son as the Good Shepherd will lay down his life for the sheep to take it up again (10:15). All of these sayings, however, do not deal with the love that should exist among the disciples. Instead of teaching two commandments, the author tells his followers that Jesus demands only one:

> A new commandment I give to you that you love one another; even as I have loved you, you also love one another. By this all men will know that you are my disciples if you have love for one another (13:34–35).

What the author of First John directs to his readers further clarifies the meaning of this one commandment:

> If anyone says I love God and hates his brother, he is a liar; for he who does not love his brother whom he has seen, cannot love God whom he has not seen (1 Jn 4:20).

The author of the gospel knows that the love of God and neighbor belong together but emphasizes that it is through the love of the brethren that believers can love God. The "new commandment" of the Johannine community does not mean the love command itself but the criteria by which the community will judge that love. No longer does the believer love the neighbor as self. The follower of Jesus must love the brethren as Jesus loved them. Since Jesus was the Good Shepherd who gave his life for the sheep, the follower of Jesus must love the brethren to the point of dying for a single member of the community.

The author also omits any reference to the love of the enemy. The members of the Johannine community love the brethren, those who are members of the community. Unless the followers are joined together in a bond of love, flowing from the bond of faith that joins the individuals to Jesus, they will be unable to fulfill the further mission of Christianity to the world. This sectarian community, which saw itself as different from other Christian communities, banded together for mutual support and protection; following the example of the Lord they would willingly give up their lives for the sake of the brethren. If the parable of the Good Shepherd exemplified the faith relationship between Jesus and the individual believer, the parable of the Vine and the Branches completes this faith dimension by teaching the followers to bear fruit, to love one another.

■ **The Good Shepherd and the Vine and the Branches** ■

These two parables—the Good Shepherd and the Vine and the Branches—are frequently compared. They have a similarity in structure and in theology. Both present a parable followed by an explanation, but the more significant comparison lies in the theology. Both parables manifest the close relationship between Jesus and the individual, with the first stressing the faith dimension. The parable of the Vine and the Branches emphasizes the finality of faith: the love of the brethren. This parable expands and explains the love of the brethren in chapter 13.

The parable of the Vine and the Branches opens with a recognition formula, an identification of Jesus as the true vine, along with a reference to the activity of God the Father. God the Father calls disciples to faith. Here the Father prunes and cuts the branches to make them more fruitful. The meaning of fruitfulness, however, does not become clear until verse 12. In the opening verses of the parable the chief participants are presented and interrelated: the Father who loves Jesus and who brings individuals to Jesus; the Son who loves the Father and his disciples; and finally the disciples themselves, as the branches that bear fruit by loving one another.

Faith Presupposed in Love

Unlike the parable of the Good Shepherd, which centers on faith, this parable presupposes faith: "You are already made clean by the word I have spoken to you" (15:3). The disciples already are related to the Lord by their faith commitment. The Lord now reminds them to remain close to him. With faith as the presupposition, the author can concentrate on the result of faith: the love of the brethren.

Love of the Brethren

The interpretation of the parable from verse 7 to 17 clarifies the need for love as the fulfillment of the command of Jesus and makes evident the responsibility to give one's life for a member of the community. Faith becomes authentic only when it leads to love of Jesus (15:9–10) and the love one for another (15:12–17). Only through the presence of love in the community can the mission of Jesus continue. The author juxtaposes both faith and love with mission, implying that the internal life of the community and its mission to the world are inseparable. If the believer wishes to fulfill the call to discipleship, this will be possible only through an internal love for the brethren, which includes a willingness to give one's life for the community:

> This is my commandment, that you love one another as I have loved you. Greater love has no man than this, that a man lay down his life for his friends. You are my friends if you do what I command you (15:12–14).

The final verse sums up what Jesus has been saying. He returns to his simple command: "This I command you, to love one another" (15:17).

Life Through Jesus

The parable stresses first of all the individual relationship to Jesus. While the word *life* is not mentioned, the notion is understood. Jesus is the source of life for the branches, and so they must remain in him. No apparent relationship exists among the branches. That relationship becomes evident only later. All receive their life from Jesus, the vine, and then each glorifies God by bearing fruit. The parable also contains the warning that a branch can be cut off and burned. Such an event has no effect on the other branches, which continue to remain united with Jesus. The individual must remain in Jesus.

The individual figures prominently in this parable, as well as in the Good Shepherd parable. The relationship of individuals within the community then becomes clearer. The command of Jesus to love one another binds the community together. The power of love moves from God to Jesus to the disciples, with the culmination in the mutual love of disciple for disciple. Faith finds its completion not only in the love of the Lord but also in the love of the brethren.

These two parables bear the witness of the Johannine community to the essentials of Christianity: the community must rest its foundation on a personal commitment of faith to Jesus, and this faith must bear fruit. Without the personal acceptance of Jesus and the fulfillment of the command of love, there can be no Christian church. Faith and love found everything and sustain everything. When present, all things are possible. When absent, Christianity ceases to exist.

■ Johannine Mysticism ■

Please read John 14:1–31.

In chapter 15 the author interplays the "abiding with," or "being with" with the disciples and Jesus, and Jesus and God, and the disciples and God. Some call this "Johannine mysticism." The same notion appears in the farewell discourses, especially in chapters 14 and 17. The author implies a mystical union between Jesus and God. The chapters also imply some sense of future union that will involve all participants:

> A little while now and the world will see me no more; but you will see me as one who has life, and you will have life (14:19).

Because this author was aware of the importance of the present moment, this union was not divorced from history. The abiding of God through Jesus culminates and completes the fellowship made possible through faith. The future union was present in the earthly relationship between Jesus and his disciples. The fellowship had begun but would be perfected in a more intimate union when Jesus had been glorified:

> If anyone loves me he will keep my word and my Father will love him and we will come to him and make our home with him (14:23).

Those who responded in faith entered into a special type of knowledge and love with Jesus and with God the Father. The union joined not just the revealer, and those to whom he revealed God, but the very source of the revelation and the revelation itself: God the Father.

Farewell Discourses and Johannine Mysticism

Please read John 13:31—14:31; 15:12—16:33.

The need for a fruitful life of love on the part of the believers appears in other sections of the gospel (chapters 13–17). Mystical union and interiority appear in the first section of these discourses (13:31–14:31), while exterior expression and witness characterize the second section (15:12–16:33). In the first section the command of love figures prominently, continuing the command of 13:34. The author repeats it again in 15:12. The intervening verses stress mutual indwelling. Thirteen out of the fourteen times the author uses the word meaning "to remain in" occur in this first section. The mutual indwelling of Father and Son, and Jesus and his disciples, occurs seven times.

Chapter 14 begins with the call to the disciples to believe in Jesus as they have believed in God and promises that the goal of the journey is God the Father (14:12). Through Jesus the disciples also will reach the Father and be with God (14:6–23).

Chapter 15 continues the theme of mutual indwelling in spite of its abrupt ending. The development comes from a change in perspective. The author introduces the bearing of fruit as a result of the abiding in Jesus. The section climaxes in verse 10:

> You will live in my love if you keep my commandments,
> even as I have kept my Father's commandments, and live
> in his love (15:10).

The focus of union and indwelling is the love of Jesus for his disciples, rooted in the love of God for Jesus and then for his followers. Johannine mysticism does not conclude in a sterile union but an abiding presence that rests on responsible love directed outward to the brethren. Finally, the author sees the love as the perfection and the completion of the union already present. Seeing and believing become knowing and loving and, ultimately, uniting and testifying.

■ The Essentials of Christianity ■

The church results from belief in Jesus, which accomplishes a union of hearts and wills with God. The same love that binds Jesus to the Father binds the Father to the followers and the followers to each other. The one commandment of the Johannine gospel is possible because in its observance the individual experiences the love of God. Johannine mysticism, the relationship and union with God, demands a union of love among the brethren. Interiority becomes externalized in the community of believers. Faith founds Christianity, but this faith of necessity moves to the love of the brethren, which then includes the love of God, for all are united.

The World

The need for a united community becomes more evident in contrast to the world. The section on hatred of the world (15:18–16:4) follows immediately after the mutual love explanation of the parable of the Vine and the Branches. The juxtaposition of these themes relates the stance of the disciples to the world and to that of Jesus himself. Jesus was rejected. The disciples will be rejected for the same reason: "They do not know the one who sent me" (16:3); the disciples will be expelled from the synagogue (16:2) and will be put to death (16:2b) "because they knew neither the Father nor me" (16:3).

Jesus prepared his followers for rejection and persecution, but only after he had made them secure in his love and the love of God. In the first section of the farewell discourses Jesus asks his disciples to deepen their personal assimilation in faith to him as God's Son. The second half presents the disciples growing in their union with Jesus in his personal relationship to the Father and in his mission from the Father to the world. The love they bear one for another will be the sustaining power for them to continue this mission.

Previously the author presented the orientation in faith as the work of God the Father. The same idea occurs in the first section of the farewell discourses, recalling the earlier statement: "No one can come to me unless the Father who sent me, draws him" (6:44). In these final words before Jesus departs, the love that the disciples have for each other also has its origin in the love of God as Father:

> For the Father himself loves you from the fact that you have loved me and have believed that I have come forth from the side of God. (16:27).

The disciples' knowledge of God, through love, leads them to recognize the nature of God. This also explains the presence of only one commandment in the gospel of John, as well as the emphasis in 1 John on the need to love one another.

Faith and Love

The union of Jesus with his disciples through faith and love, the command of love and the witness of the followers in the world interact. They make the Christian community different from any other type of religious community. For the author of this gospel, faith and love are essential. When they are present, Jesus the Lord, his Spirit and the Father are present. When these qualities are absent, there can be no Christian church, for they alone make a Christian community possible.

The role of faith, the command of love and the mystical union that the author emphasizes in his gospel are all elements of the church. The evangelist does not present a complete ecclesiology in this gospel. Rather, he chose to present to his readers those elements that he saw as foundational for the church. For the Christian community of all ages the Johannine community continues to bear testimony to the essentials of Christianity. Everything the church possesses or operates or directs must have its foundation in the personal commitment to the Lord and the love of the brethren. Only then can the church fulfill its mission to all.

Suggestions for Reflection

1. Do you think faith and love are the only essentials of Christianity? What do you think of the need for authority?
2. The gospel is individualistic. What are the advantages and disadvantages of this stress on individualism?
3. If you have to love only the brethren, does this make the church of this gospel somewhat hypocritical? Is it not better to also love your enemies?
4. Jesus calls his followers by name. Why does this give comfort?
5. Do you like the image of the Good Shepherd, even if most believers live in urban societies?
6. The parable of the Vine and the Branches joins love to faith. Why are they so united?
7. Is a union between God and Jesus and then between Jesus and his followers important? How does this bring about a unity of God with all people?
8. Be especially careful of love. Why?

4.

The Prologue

Please read John 1:1–18.

*M*ost Christians have a deep affection for the opening verses of the gospel of John, perhaps especially older Christians. This gospel was read at the conclusion of every Mass up to the reform of the Second Vatican Council. Poetry always seems to lift the human spirit higher than prose, and these verses are surely poetry.

The original poem may have circulated outside the community of the Fourth Gospel, or it may have been the creation of this community. Probably the poem was first a hymn to Wisdom, which then became a hymn to the Word. Jesus is not only the Word of God Incarnate but also the Wisdom of God Incarnate. Both ideas exist behind the poem.

When the author of the gospel incorporated the poem into the gospel he added certain verses that clearly destroy the flow of ideas and the rhythm. The comments on John in verses 6–9 and verse 15 were probably added to counteract the influence that the Baptizer still held among some early Jews and perhaps some early Christians.

The Poem and Wisdom

The poem also has some relationship to the eighth chapter of Proverbs, which glorifies God's Wisdom. In an Old Testament tradition Wisdom is the order God has implanted in the universe. When people discover Wisdom, the order or plan of God, all will be well. When people disregard the order established by God, then all will suffer.

Jesus is the Wisdom of God who reveals God's plan for creation and for all people. Jesus offers guidance and direction for human life. When people follow this Wisdom, they follow the light and they experience true life. When individuals refuse to recognize the Wisdom of God in Jesus, they must suffer the consequences.

Like other hymns of the New Testament this one speaks of the descent and implies an ascent in the closing verse 18. In Philippians 2 for example, Jesus descends but then is exalted. Here the Word of God descends and becomes part of human history. The mighty Word of God, while all was in darkness, came from heaven and became flesh.

> When peaceful silence lay over all, and night had run the half of her swift course, down from the heavens, from the royal throne, leapt your all-powerful Word (Wis 18:14–15).

■ The Theology of the Word ■

The author uses the title *Logos* or Word only in the prologue of the gospel, and the title is used only in verse 1 and verse 14. Once the Word has become flesh, the emphasis shifts to Jesus, who is the incarnation and personification of the one Word of God. While the title is no longer used in the gospel, the theology behind the word dominates the gospel. *To speak* occurs fifty-nine times throughout this gospel, connoting a solemn speaking on the part of Jesus that demands a listening and a response.

When Jesus speaks solemnly he speaks of his word here on earth and about his special relationship to God and his mission. Who he is and what he does form the content of the principal words of Jesus. In chapters 7 and 8 the verb *to speak* is used seventeen times. Jesus reveals himself solemnly during the feast of Tabernacles, and he reveals his mission to all people. Jesus will give eternal life to all who come to him and drink.

In the gospel the disciples listen to the Word. To be a follower of the Lord one must hear what Jesus has to say (7:40); accept his word (12:48) and remain in his word (8:31). With whoever believes in Jesus, the Word abides (5:38), and this Word gives spirit and life (6:63), especially eternal life (12:50).

■ The Origin of the *Logos*, the "Word" ■

In the past some scholars tried to show that the concept of *Logos*—Word—contained in the prologue came from the influence of Greek philosophy. A study of ancient Greek philosophy shows that the *logos* was often seen as the stable element in a world of flux, or as the primary power or rational order in the universe. This also included guidance for ethical behavior.

■ Judaism and Philosophy ■

Logos was also an important concept, with a long and complex history, in Hellenistic Judaism. The Wisdom of Solomon, a Hellenistic-Jewish text from the first century B.C.E. explicitly connects wisdom and *logos*. The Jewish-Hellenistic philosopher Philo also identified *logos* with wisdom. For this philosopher, *logos* was the intermediary reality between God and the universe. *Logos* was the image of God, and the *logos* gave guidance to the human soul to reach the divine realm. The possibility of the human soul to know God and experience the vision of God, according to Philo, was based on the soul's fundamental relationship to and participation in the divine *logos*. The divine *logos,* related to the human soul, was the means by which the human soul mystically rose above the material world to contemplate the divine *logos* and even God.

Old Testament Origins

No one need study philosophy, however, to understand the fundamental source for *Word* in the New Testament. In Genesis God "said," and it was. In Isaiah 55:10–11 the Word effects change. In Proverbs 8:22 Wisdom was created in the beginning and was near to God as a confidant and a fellow-worker in creation. Jewish speculation about Wisdom and God's Word gives more than enough material to understand how the author of the prologue could have composed or used a hymn that could be adapted perfectly to apply to Jesus as the Word of God Incarnate.

Memra

The Aramaic Targums (a type of popular commentary) on the Pentateuch use the *memra* (Word) of God more than six hundred times. The *memra* creates, reveals and saves. Commenting on Genesis 14:19, 22 the author of a Targum remarks that the *memra* of God created the heavens and the earth. In Deuteronomy people live by everything that has been created by the *memra*. In paradise Adam and Eve heard the voice of the *memra*. Enoch is taken up by the *memra,* and the covenant of Genesis 9:12 is stipulated between the *memra* and the patriarch. In the Exodus the *memra* plays the role of liberator both by saving Israel and by punishing Egypt.

The Palestinian Targums also attribute to the *memra* different divine actions and reactions that the Bible attributes to God alone. God acts and communicates through the *memra*. The *memra* is not a substitute God but rather a way in which God becomes present to Israel in a personal manner.

The Prologue of the Fourth Gospel

Probably all of the above influences helped create the prologue of the Gospel According to John. Fundamentally the foundation may have been speculation on Jewish Wisdom but also might have included some of the elements from Hellenistic Judaism and even of incipient Gnosticism.

■   The Literary Structure   ■

The literary structure of the prologue often is likened to a parabola: The Word in the first verse is with God, descends to become flesh in verse 14, but remains with God the Father in verse 18. The whole poem has an established framework and a repetition of ideas that also find expression throughout the gospel.

The prologue offers an overture to the entire gospel. Many of the themes contained in the body of the gospel find their first presentation here. Light and darkness; life giving through faith; acceptance and rejection; the closeness of Jesus to God—all are found within the prologue.

The Individual Verses

In the beginning was the Word and the Word
was with God and the Word was God (1:1).

In verse 1 the words "in the beginning" may have some reference to the opening verse of Genesis. In this gospel the author deals with a beginning that precedes the beginning of creation. Also this verse demonstrates the closeness of Word and God by the phrase "with God." The Greek preposition connotes a nearness of persons that would never have been used in reference to God. No one is closer to God than the Word. Also in this verse the author refers to the Word as God. Unfortunately, the English language does not offer the subtlety of Greek. In Greek the word for God, *theos,* is always used with the definite article when it refers to God the Father, *o theos.* When Greek wishes to express divinity it can use an adjective, *theion,* or it can choose to hold a middle position and use the noun, *theos,* but without the article. This verse really says: In the beginning was the Word and the Word was with God and the Word was God (no article). In this way the author speaks of the Word as being as close to God as possible but does not completely identify the two. Jesus is equal to God and also dependent upon God.

He was in the beginning with God (1:2).

Verse 2 may well be a repetition or even an addition to the poem, adding little to what precedes or follows.

All things were made through him and without
him was not anything made that was made (1:3).

Verse 3 shows the role of the Word in creation. The Word was active in creation and actually entered into the act. The Word creates as God's Son and creates all things so nothing can ever be seen as evil. All is good because all is created by God and the Word. All creation also bears the stamp of God and so reveals God. God offers a relationship to people through creation but especially through Jesus the Son of God. Perhaps here the author also offers a subtle apology against any one who would denigrate the material in favor of the spiritual.

In him was life, and the life was the light of men (1:4).

Verse 4 relates the Word to people. The Word is the mediator of God's most precious gifts: life and light. What makes a person a person is the gift of life, that which a person shares with all living things. What distinguishes people from animals is intelligence or rationality or light. This verse also contains a problem of translation. Should the verse be translated "that which had come to be was life in him" or "that which had come to be in him was life"? Opinions line up on both sides.

The light shines in the darkness and the darkness has not
overcome it (1:5).

Verse 5 shows a change in time in the poetic measure and may not pertain to the original hymn. However, it echoes a frequent theme of the gospel: the conflict between light and darkness, between good and evil, and it carries the conviction that the darkness will never defeat the light or understand the light. Nicodemus comes from the darkness to see Jesus (3:2) and Judas returns to the darkness when he decides to go through with the betrayal (13:30)

> There was a man sent from God whose name was John.
> He came for testimony, to bear witness to the light, that
> all might believe through him.
> He was not the light, but came to bear witness to the
> light (1:6–8).

Verses 6, 7 and 8 are clear additions and can be understood as a clever apologetic against those who still thought of John the Baptizer as the messiah. He was not the light but came to bear testimony to the light. His function becomes clearer in the second part of this chapter, when John explicitly announces that he points others to Jesus.

> The true light that enlightens every man was coming into the
> world (1:9).

Verse 9 is the continuation of verse 4, completing the idea of giving enlightenment as well as giving fife.

> He was in the world and the world and the world was
> made through him, yet the world knew him not.
> He came to his own home and his own people received him not
> (1:10–11).

Verses 10 and 11 are poignant: the world did not recognize the Word and even his very own (a favorite expression with the author) do not recognize the Word. People had been prepared for the coming of God's Word in human form since the Word had been expressed in creation and proclaimed in the history of Israel, but in spite of this preparation those expected to recognize the Word—his very own people—did not. The Jewish people had received God's Word. Its leaders had studied this Word, but unfortunately many did not recognize the Word of God in Jesus.

> But to all who received him, who believed in his name, he
> gave power to become children of God (1:12).

Verse 12 returns to a happy refrain: many did accept him, even if some did not. The emphasis in this verse centers not on any ethical activity but rather on people recognizing what they truly are, God's children. They are only to believe in the name of the Lord and that in itself will bring them to a realization of their destiny, to be God's family. God gave them the power to see in Jesus the eternal Word, and God also gave them power to accept this Word and receive life.

> Who were born, not of blood nor of the will of man but of God (1:13).

Verse 13 continues the thought of verse 12. God the Father is the one who will bring people to faith. No human power alone can accomplish this great gift. To be born of the power of God, and that alone, brings salvation.

Textually this verse offers an interesting problem. Some of the later Latin manuscripts—and some other earlier manuscript witnesses as well—have a singular verb in this verse rather than a plural. If a singular verb is original, then the verb refers not to those coming to faith but to the Word himself who is born. This singular verb would then be seen as having reference to the birth of the Word made flesh, not from blood or the will of the flesh or the will of man, but by God. Could this possibly be a reference to the virginal conception of Jesus? For those who hold that the singular verb is original, that is the only response. The problem, however, remains. Not one of the early Greek manuscripts has a singular verb; they all have a plural, and it is easier to understand why a scribe would change a plural verb to a singular (to bring this gospel into accord with the witness of Luke and Matthew to the virginal conception) than to understand why a scribe would change a singular to a plural. This textual problem illustrates well what good scriptural scholarship must accomplish. An additional textual problem is the word for blood. Actually in Greek it is plural, giving interpreters a field day in trying to offer a satisfactory explanation.

> And the Word became flesh and dwelt among us, full of grace and truth; we have beheld his glory, glory of the only Son from the Father (1:14).

Verse 14 culminates the hymn. The Word pitched his tent among us. The imagery is reminiscent of the Old Testament tradition in which God is present in a tabernacle that is portable and can be carried wherever the people travel. The Word will be with his people no matter where they go. The notion of tent also connotes a temporary presence. The Word will be with humanity as incarnate only for a time. It must return to where it belongs and indeed whence it has

never left. When the Word has returned, the disciples will experience the Spirit, who will take up a permanent indwelling with those
who have become children of God through faith.

Wisdom also pitches her tent:

> Then the creator of all gave me his command and he who
> formed me chose the spot for my tent. Saying: In Jacob
> make your dwelling (Sir 24:8).

The Hebrew words for "to pitch a tent" and "to dwell" are very similar; only an addition of an "h" distinguishes them. The author plays
on the words *tent* and *dwelling*. The Word will dwell with his people,
and the Word will be present as incarnate and as Wisdom giving
guidance and direction. The translation "among" us really should be
translated "in" us. The Word enters into human history and will
enter into everyone who responds in faith.

Flesh

The use of "flesh" in this verse also may make some reference to
the death of Jesus. The prologue contains many of the major themes
of the gospel, and it would be surprising if the author did not include
some reference to the glorification of Jesus through his death on the
cross. The Greek word for flesh, *sarx,* can carry a sacrificial overtone.
On the cross the Word made flesh offers himself for the sake of others so that they may become more faithful. The offering of Jesus
reveals the glory of God and the glory of God's Son. God's goodness
and fidelity become most evident in the death of Jesus.

Glory

The reference to glory in this verse also strikes a familiar
theme of the gospel. The glory of God in the Old Testament is
always the manifestation of goodness and power. This manifestation, moreover, brings together the covenantal virtues *hesed* and
emeth, "mercy" and "fidelity," which also can be translated in English as "grace" and "truth." In the Word Become Flesh true believers have seen the power and goodness of God. They have seen the
compassion of God, the kindness, the forgiveness and the fidelity
of God, for Jesus has made these divine qualities visible in human
form.

> John bore witness to him and cried, "This was he of
> whom I said, 'He who comes after me ranks before me, for
> he was before me'" (1:15).

Verse 15 is another addition continuing the reference to John the Baptizer. It reinforces the teaching that John fulfills his ministry by giving testimony.

> And from his fullness we have all received, grace upon grace
> (1:16).

Verse 16 completes the thought of verse 14. There is a superabundance of God's graciousness for all—that which the Word has received and that which the Word imparts.

> For the law was given through Moses; grace and truth came
> through Jesus Christ (1:17).

Verse 17 should be seen as another addition, an editorial comment on verse 16.

> No one has ever seen God; the only Son, who is in the
> bosom of the Father, he has made him known (1:18).

The final verse has the Word with the Father. The Word has completed his mission of revealing God the Father to all who will respond and has never left God while so doing. The Word has become flesh and has also become the Son to the one Father of all, making him also the brother of all.

The theology of the prologue includes the basic thought of the gospel: Jesus, the Word Become Flesh, reveals God the Father. He has come into a dark and evil world and has offered to people the possibility of moving from darkness to light. Those who accept the offer become part of God's family. Jesus accomplished his revelation by manifesting God's glory through his mercy and fidelity. His earliest followers saw him for a while and came to believe in him as God's Son. The divine Word took on the flesh common to all and directed to death, so that all may respond humanly in faith to the offering of eternal life by the God of all.

As the gospel unfolds the reader comes to appreciate these basic themes at greater depth. The evangelist will return repeatedly to the same offer of faith, each time deepening its meaning and drawing more people into its realm of influence. The great overture of the gospel ends, to be repeated in ever stronger overtones throughout the gospel.

Suggestions for Reflection

1. Jesus as the Word is with God but differs from God. How does this affect your understanding of Jesus? Your prayer life?

2. Can Jesus be equal to the Father and still not equal? Is this not a contradiction?

3. What role did the Word play in creation? Is the Word the example after which all was created?

4. Light and life are necessary for human life. Where do light and life originate, according to the prologue? How does Jesus give life and light?

5. The witness to the Baptist in the prologue places the Baptist on a different plane when compared to Jesus. What role does the Baptist play here and in the rest of the gospel?

6. "The Word became flesh and made his dwelling in us" describes many aspects of Johannine theology. Why are the ideas important for understanding the Johannine Jesus?

7. Grace and truth are Old Testament concepts. In examining them, how would you relate them to the meaning of Christianity?

8. Jesus as the Word never leaves the Father. What implications are found in this statement?

9. The prologue offers themes that will recur in the gospel. What basic gospel themes can you find in this prologue?

10. Is the prologue a good introduction to the gospel?

5.

The Sacraments in the Fourth Gospel

The Fourth Gospel contains many sacramental images. The presence or absence of references to the sacraments in the Fourth Gospel, however, need not be identified with the sacramental symbolism. The debate has occupied scholars for years. Some find references to the sacraments throughout the gospel, while others deny any reference. But no one doubts the sacramental aspects in this gospel. The author filled his gospel with symbolism and images that remind the listener or reader of the presence of the spiritual or the divine. But can these sacramental references pertain in any way to the Christian sacraments? Moreover, if the gospel emphasizes so strongly the need for personal faith, then what role might sacraments play? Are there clear references to baptism and the eucharist, and if so, how are these sacraments presented in this gospel?

■ Baptism ■

The author of this gospel certainly knew Christian baptism. He alluded to the baptism of Jesus, even though he chose not to narrate the event. The dialogue with Nicodemus contains some reference to baptism; other references to water (the blind man in chapter 9, the foot washing in chapter 13, and the water from the side of Christ in chapter 19) might carry some baptismal overtones.

John's Baptism

Please read John 1:19–36; 3:22–36.

The allusion to the baptism of Jesus in chapter 1 and the final witness of John to Jesus (3:22–26) seem to show the author's interest in the new baptism of the Spirit over against the water baptism

67

of John. He implies that John actually baptized Jesus, especially
when this account is compared with that of the synoptics. Still, he
does not mention an actual baptism by water. Verses 26 and 33 clarify the position of the author when he has John the Baptizer distinguish his baptism from the messianic baptism of the Spirit.

> John answered them: "I baptize with water, but among
> you stands one whom you do not know, even he who
> comes after me, the thong of whose sandal I am unworthy
> to untie." He on whom you see the Spirit descend and
> remain, this is he who baptizes in the Holy Spirit.

In verse 32 the Spirit descends and remains on Jesus, a distinctive
characteristic of the messiah. No definite conclusions can be drawn
from these texts regarding baptism other than the general notion
that in the context in which the author could have mentioned the
actual baptism of Jesus, he did not. Rather, he chose to emphasize
the coming of the Spirit on Jesus and the remaining of the Spirit on
Jesus. The context implies baptism, but the text ignores the actual
ritual of baptism.

The Dialogue with Nicodemus

Please read John 3:1–15.
The dialogue with Nicodemus also seems to have reference to
baptism. The burden of Jesus' remarks, however, concerns the
entering into the kingdom of God by being born from above (or
again) and being begotten of the Spirit. Those who seek God must
be born from above; the flesh can beget flesh while spirit begets
spirit. If an individual desires to move from the natural level of life
to the divine level, then God must do the raising. Just as in the creation of humankind God breathed the Spirit into the lifeless form to
give life, so in this new creation the new gift of life must be communicated through the divine Spirit. Jesus can communicate this life-
giving Spirit because he is the heavenly Son of Man who has
descended from heaven (3:13).

Begetting by the Spirit

The primary meaning of the text does not refer to baptism of
water but to the eschatological begetting through the outpouring

of the Spirit of God made possible through Jesus. Nicodemus could have understood the reference to the outpouring of the Spirit since it frequently occurs the Old Testament (Is 4:4; Zec 12:10; 13:1; Ez 36:25–27), but he seems to be unaware of this tradition.

Throughout the gospel references are made to the relationship between the coming of the Spirit and water. Here in the dialogue the author compares the Spirit to the wind (a play on words since in Greek the same word can be translated "spirit" or "wind"). The extended discourse by Jesus emphasizes the role and the meaning of the Spirit. A reference to baptism by water could hardly be understood in the full dialogue.

"Water and the Spirit"

One verse, however, does seem to imply water baptism: "No one can enter into God's kingdom without being begotten of water and Spirit" (3:5). This should be contrasted with John 3:3: "No one can see the reign of God unless he is begotten from above"; and also with John 3:8: "So it is with everyone begotten of the Spirit." The presence of "water and" in verse 5, when compared to the general meaning of the dialogue, has encouraged some exegetes to conclude that these words are an addition. No early manuscript evidence, however, supports such an opinion. Some argue for a baptismal tone by claiming that faith in the Son of Man must be made concrete in the act of water baptism. Others recognize the tenuous status of the words "water and" within the theology of the dialogue and argue that this verse existed in the tradition of the evangelist but without a reference to water prior to the composition of the gospel. The evangelist added "water and" to make the text speak of baptism and bring the saying into accord with the general practice of the early church, which was performing water baptism. The gospel can lay claim to faith as necessary for baptism and vice versa.

The "no one can" expression in both verses 3 and 5 might be related to the earlier comment by Nicodemus concerning Jesus: "No one can do these signs that you do unless God is with him" (3:2). The reference to the kingdom of God not only refers to the goal of Christian life but also to the means of entering that realm, the eternal life made possible through Jesus.

Water and Spirit in the Scripture

The Old Testament often combines water and spirit. Both Ezekiel and Isaiah join them:

> I will sprinkle clean water on you...a new heart I will give you and a new spirit will I pour within you (Ez 36:25–27).

> I will pour out water on the thirsty land, and streams on the dry ground; I will pour my Spirit upon your descendants and my blessing on your offspring. They shall spring up like grass among waters (Is 44:3–4).

Water was frequently used as a metaphor for the Spirit and the Fourth Gospel also recognizes this:

> Out of this heart shall flow rivers of living water. Now this he said about the Spirit which those who believed in him were to receive; for as yet the Spirit had not been given because Jesus was not yet glorified (7:38–39).

Some see water and spirit as parallel ideas. Water refers to physical birth, and spirit refers to spiritual birth. This parallel then continues in the following verses referring to flesh and spirit.

The likelihood that verse 5 refers to water baptism in some way seems acceptable, but the text stipulates baptism as a means of birth only through faith. The question of whether the words "water and" were not originally part of the gospel or the tradition but added to the gospel in its composition remains debatable. Certainly the gospel did not circulate without these words, since no early manuscript evidence supports this opinion and since often those who favor such an opinion do so for ideological reasons. The following position seems attractive: somewhere in the process of the Johannine tradition the rebirth by the Spirit, the fundamental meaning of the text, became associated with the act of water baptism. The text does contain a reference to water baptism but it belongs to a tradition that emerged later in the Johannine community. The earliest tradition emphasized the role of the Spirit and faith. Since this is primary, water baptism alone never suffices. The community shares the general practice of early Christianity of baptism by water but chose to emphasize that baptism in the Spirit remains primary. The individual shares in this coming of the Spirit by faith.

The Feast of Tabernacles/
Water from the Side of Jesus

Please read John 7:37–39; 19:34.

The feast of Tabernacles or Booths celebrated the harvest with a service in the temple. On the last day of the feast a vessel of water was brought from the pool of Siloam and poured out before the altar of burnt offerings. With the blowing of the horns and trumpets the people gave thanks for rain. The drawing of water on this feast reminded the worshipers of the life-giving water given to them by God through Moses when the people were dying from thirst (Ex 17:1–6). The feast also anticipated the abundant gift of water flowing from Jerusalem in the kingdom of God (Is 12:3; Ez 47:1–12; Zec 14:8) and the hope for sufficient water for the years's crops.

On the feast of Tabernacles Jesus stood up and cried:

> "If anyone thirsts, let him come to me; let him drink who
> believes in me. Scripture has it: 'From within him rivers
> of living water shall flow'" (7:37–38).

Some Bibles may have a slight variation from this text because of a difference in punctuation. The verse can also read:

> "Let him come and let him drink. He who believes in him,
> as scripture has it, from within him shall flow rivers of
> living water."

From whom does the living water flow—from Jesus or from the believer? Or does the author wish to imply that it flows from both? The verse continues with reference to the Spirit. The author informs his readers that Jesus was speaking of the Spirit, which was yet to be given since Jesus had not yet been glorified (7:39). These verses refer not to water baptism but to the gift of the Spirit that will be given on Calvary.

The flow of water from the side of Jesus in chapter 19:34 and the handing over of his Spirit to the Beloved Disciple and his mother in chapter 19:26–27 can be seen as the fulfillment of the prediction in chapter 7. Water in chapter 7, then, refers to the Spirit. This interpretation need not seem odd since, as already noted, often in the Old Testament water designated the Spirit. Obviously, however, the water in chapter 7 cannot be immediately identified with baptismal water. The early fathers of the church did indeed see in this text a reference to baptism, but that may not prove such was the intention of the author of the gospel.

In the seventh chapter the evangelist interrupted his narrative to remark that by water, Jesus meant the Spirit, which followers would receive after he had been glorified. The flow of water from his side, from within him, fulfilled this prophecy, since it takes place when he is glorified. Verse 35 with reference to belief relates this flow of water from Jesus' side to that of the seventh chapter and the call to faith. Again the author of this gospel joins the Spirit and faith to the symbolism of water.

Blood from the Side of Jesus

The reference to blood from Jesus' side causes more problems. The remarks in the First Epistle of John (5:6–8) join the elements of water, blood and spirit with testimony. For the author of this gospel, and for the author of the epistle, the baptism by John did not give the Spirit. The real begetting from water and the Spirit was accomplished only when Jesus was glorified (7:39). But the Spirit could not be given until Jesus had departed (16:7), until he had died or had shed his blood. In the phrase in the epistle, the water had to be mingled with the blood before the Spirit could give testimony. Thus, in the gospel picture of the flow of blood and water from the side of Christ, the author informs his readers that now the Spirit can be given because Jesus has died and through his death he has gained the glory that was his before the world began (17:5). The thrusting of the lance demonstrated the truth of his death and made the affirmation of death the paradoxical beginning of life. From the dead Jesus comes forth living water, the Spirit, to all who will believe in him. The Beloved Disciple and the mother of Jesus stand at the foot of the cross to receive this Spirit.

The author of this gospel relates the pouring forth of the water from the side of Christ in prophecy (7:37–39) and in actuality (19:34) to the gift of the Spirit that Jesus gave when glorified. Since, however, the gift of the Spirit was associated with baptism in the Johannine community (3:3), the author may refer to baptism at least obliquely. Also, the mention of water alone would bring to mind such an association for the early church. The meaning of the life-giving Spirit accepted in faith remains the dominant theme, even if some references can be found to water baptism.

■ The Blind Man ■

Please read John 9:1–41.

The blind man figures as a representative figure in this gospel. The reference to water in this chapter may not at first sight seem very sacramental in tone. Clearly the early church interpreted this chapter as baptismal, but does the text give any hints as to the accuracy of that interpretation?

The Miracle

The evangelist narrates the miracle in only two verses. The rest of the chapter is dialogue concerning those who truly see, or those who truly believe in Jesus. The author describes the gestures of Jesus, but the man sees only when he actually washes in the pool. Since the man's physical blindness contrasts with the sin of spiritual blindness (9:39) and the evangelist emphasized that the man had been born blind (9:1, 2, 13, 18–19, 20, 24), the author seems to be playing on the idea that the man was born in sin (9:2, 34). Even if Jesus denies such a charge (9:3) this sin of blindness can be removed only by bathing in the water of the pool of Siloam.

The Pool

The author also pauses to explain the meaning of the name of the pool: "one who has been sent." Since in this gospel Jesus is the one who has been sent by the Father (3:17, 34; 5:36, etc.) the pool becomes associated with Jesus in the mind of the evangelist and then in the minds of the readers. Water from this pool was used during the Jewish feast of Tabernacles, a harvest feast, and on that occasion Jesus had remarked that he was the source of life-giving water. All these elements interact within the chapter, making the episode much more involved than just a healing of a blind man.

The man in sin must be washed in the pool. Here and only here does the evangelist afford power to the water—but not in a magical sense, since the use of the interpretation of the word *Siloam* binds the water to Jesus himself. The implicit reference to the feast of

Tabernacles further emphasizes the role of Jesus in accomplishing the healing of the man. He needed to be washed to be healed. Jesus caused the healing and used water. The baptismal overtones are strong, but once again, the place of faith remains primary.

■   The Foot Washing   ■

Please read John 13:1–20.

The foot washing has always been understood as sacramental but not necessarily in the sense of one of the sacraments. The impetus to seek some special sacramental meaning comes not from the choice of words or the context but rather from the importance given to the foot washing by Jesus. Without sharing in the foot washing his disciples can have no share in his heritage (13:8). The act of humiliation does not suffice to secure participation in his heritage. This element in the chapter has encouraged scholars to find some special sacramental implication in the event, but is that the only possible explanation?

The Meaning of the Foot Washing

Since Jesus said he must wash Peter, the ritual is not simply an example to be imitated but a salvific action of Jesus. If the foot washing can be a symbol of the salvific death of the Lord, then the importance of participating in the ritual becomes intelligible. The presence of humility must not be deleted completely since this is the interpretation given by the evangelist himself (13:14, 15) but the symbol prophesies the humiliating death of the Son of God for the forgiveness of sins. The opening statement of passing to the Father and concluding with the foot washing with the reference to the betrayal of Jesus situates the incident in the context of the death of Jesus.

Jesus provoked Peter to question him, which gave Jesus the opportunity to explain the salvific necessity of his death; dying would bring people a share in the heritage of Jesus and would cleanse them from sin. This explanation, however, still does not settle the question of some sacramental implication.

Sacramental Overtones

The mere mention of washing does not in itself connote baptism. The major meaning is soteriological, concerned with salvation.

Other allusions should not be assumed unless the text itself clearly suggests a further quest. (For example, "except for his feet" in verse 10 should not be interpreted as referring to the sacrament of penance.) The only possibility of arguing to the presence of some baptismal overtones comes not from the foot washing itself but from the meaning of the foot washing as prophesying the death of Jesus. If the death of Jesus enables him to give his Spirit (19:30b), then the reference to the death of Jesus in this passage in symbolic form, with the added claim that this accomplishes a share in his heritage, could possibly be related to baptism through association with John 7: 37–39 and 3:5. But perhaps the stronger sacramental meaning is the eucharist. If the foot washing refers to the death of the Lord, and the eucharist has a similar salvific effect, then the foot washing can also refer to the eucharist.

In the apostolic church Spirit and water seem to have been inextricably linked very early in the development of Christianity. The close connection between water and Spirit in the Old Testament set the tone for the eventual development of the Christian sacrament of baptism. No doubt the community of the Fourth Gospel practiced water baptism. The many references to water and the close connection to the Spirit give sufficient evidence. Just as Luke in the Acts of the Apostle links water to the Spirit, to baptism, so the author of this gospel joins all three, even if the actual references to the ritual of baptism are minimal. The author of this gospel focuses his concern on the meaning rather than the ritual, on the faith of the one receiving the Spirit.

The Eucharist in the Fourth Gospel

Please read John 6:1–59.

The eucharistic interpretation of chapter 6 creates one of the most debated issues in Johannine sacramentality. Some claim a primary eucharistic meaning throughout the chapter; others admit the presence of a eucharistic tone but in a secondary mode; still others limit the eucharistic meaning to verses 51–58 and claim that these verses are from the hand of a final editor. Additional problems face the reader: Did Jesus speak the words on the historical occasion of the multiplication of the loaves, or did the evangelist construct the speech? Does the entire discourse refer to the teaching of Jesus as the Word of God with a fundamental Wisdom motif? Did the author consciously distinguish between Wisdom and eucharist in the discourse or not?

The Miracle and the Eucharist

Some eucharistic overtones appear in the miracle of the loaves. A comparison of the synoptic accounts with the Fourth Gospel demonstrates that the multiplication of the loaves was colored by the eucharistic liturgy familiar to the various early Christian communities. "To give thanks" appears in the miracle and at the Last Supper in the synoptics. Jesus himself distributes the loaves as he does the bread at the Last Supper. The use of "gather up" and the reference to the "fragments" find parallels in the eucharistic prayer of the *Didache,* an early church document.

Bread and Faith

In the first section of the discourse the bread that has come down from heaven is Jesus as the Word of God. Most will admit this. Jesus offers his word as bread, and he must be accepted in faith. The evangelist situates the teaching of Jesus in the context of messianic hopes. Another Exodus takes place, with Jesus offering the interpretation. The true bread is not the manna in the desert but what gives life to the world (6:33). Jesus, like Wisdom of old, invites all to come and recline (Prv 9: 5; Is 55:1–3). Jesus alone gives life to those who believe in him—eternal life.

Jesus expects a reaction of faith (6:35, 36, 40, 47) or a coming to him, which also means faith. In 6:45 Jesus cites Isaiah 54:13: "They shall all be taught by God," which brings out the sapiential symbolism of the bread. The nearest parallel to the bread of life is the living water in chapters 4 and 7, and water symbolizes the revelation that calls for faith.

Verses 36–40 in chapter 6 spell out the need to believe in Jesus and to accept the will of the Father that all should have life through faith. The future for people, their eschatology, also figures here; everyone who believes in the Son has eternal life even while awaiting the raising up on the last day. These themes have been present in the gospel before: God the Father works to bring individuals to Jesus, but the individual must personally accept Jesus in faith. The gift and response of faith brings eternal life *now.*

■ Eucharistic Teaching ■

The final section of the bread of life discourse proclaims that eternal life comes not only from believing but from feeding on Jesus' flesh and drinking his blood (6:54). The role of the Father recedes. Now Jesus is the principal agent for life. The vocabulary also has changed: eat, flesh, drink, blood. The stress on eating the flesh and drinking the blood cannot be a metaphor for accepting the revelation of Jesus but must refer to the eucharist. The words are too graphic and too close to the teaching on the eucharist in the early church. These words of Jesus have the same meaning as the ones recorded in the institution account of Matthew: "Take this and eat it; this is my body…drink…this is my blood" (Mt 26:26–28).

A second indication supporting the eucharistic interpretation is the formula in verse 51: "The bread I will give is my flesh, for the life of the world." This resembles the Lukan formula for institution: "This is my body to be given for you" (Lk 22:19). Even the announcement of the treason of Judas, which follows (Jn 6:71), adds another link to the Last Supper of the synoptics.

Clearly these verses are manifestations of eucharistic teaching in the gospel of John, whether they are historically related to the multiplication of the loaves or not. If, however, the first part of the chapter implies a Wisdom motif and the second part implies a eucharistic motif, what might have prompted the author to join and juxtapose the two discourses: the one, the bread of life as Wisdom demanding faith, and the other on the eucharist, which one would have expected in the farewell discourses at the Last Supper? The question appears more baffling when the reader recalls that the Fourth Gospel has the longest section on the Last Supper and makes no mention of the institution of the eucharist. Instead, the author has the eucharistic teaching in chapter 6.

The Eucharist and Faith

Some scholars suggest that the second discourse with its clear eucharistic theme serves to bring out the eucharistic meaning that is latent and secondary in the first part of the chapter. But might not the opposite be true: the first gives the meaning and the interpretation of the second? The eucharistic teaching in this chapter continues the tendency of Wisdom literature to call people to faith and involves the religious aspirations of all.

The author of the gospel presents the meaning of the eucharist as the general meaning of the coming of Jesus. Thus, the meaning of the Christian life may be summed up and expressed in the eucharist, but the eucharist can never be separated from its context: the presence in human history of Jesus as the revealer and mediator of life. People must respond to Jesus in faith made possible through the action of God the Father, who calls people to the Son. With this presupposition the eucharist can have meaning and can be the bread of life that gives eternal life to those who believe. The eucharist in the Fourth Gospel interprets the coming of Jesus himself, and vice versa. All must be accepted as the work of God the Father in giving the Son for the life of the world. The eucharist makes sense for the author of this gospel if accepted as the memorial of the redeeming incarnation. Even the eucharist takes its meaning from the fundamental christology of the Fourth Gospel, which the author always joins to the faith of those who receive it.

The Sacraments in the Fourth Gospel

The strongest reference to the ritual of baptism as a ritual is found in chapter 9 (the blind man). The discourse with Nicodemus referred originally to baptism in the Spirit and not water baptism. However, early in the Johannine tradition the baptism of water was related, at least in the consciousness of the author, to the baptism in the Spirit. The references to water in chapters 7 and 19 refer principally to the gift of the Spirit. Baptism in this gospel refers primarily to the acceptance of the Spirit and demands faith on the part of the recipient.

The only passage clearly referring to the eucharist is found in chapter 6. The eucharistic overtones of the miracle of the loaves, common to all the evangelists, sets the scene for a full eucharistic teaching in verses 51–58, but this is further interpreted by the bread of life discourse, which concentrates on faith in Jesus. Here the author also joins the celebration of the eucharist—and surely this community celebrated the Lord's Supper—irrevocably with faith.

The Fourth Gospel presents some signs of sacramental activity and teaching that might be judged explicit in their own right but must be judged as implicit when compared to the synoptics. Matthew (26:26–29), Mark (14:22–25) and Luke (22:17–20) include the institution of the eucharist at the Last Supper. This gospel does not narrate the institution, even though the author devotes four chapters to the Last Supper. Matthew also has the instruction to baptize all nations (Mt 28:19). The longer ending of Mark refers to baptism for salvation (Mk 16:16). Each records the actual baptism of Jesus by John. What might have prompted the author of John to place the sacramental activity of his community in such an oblique position? If the presence of some teaching on baptism and the eucharist seems evident, why is the ritual for both omitted?

The author of this gospel has his own peculiar interpretation of the sacraments in order to emphasize their spiritual value and to relate the sacraments to faith. The early church had many internal conflicts, and some of these early communities may have had some difficulty in dealing with the particular approach of the Johannine community. Belief in Jesus as a miracle worker never suffices for this gospel. People must believe in him as God's Son. At this period of church development a hierarchy with organization and authority and ritual was becoming commonplace. These factors coupled with the basic thrust of the gospel—the individual response of faith in Jesus as the revealer of God—help to explain the apparent lack of interest by the author of the gospel in explicit sacramental references.

■ Faith and the Sacraments ■

The presence of baptism and the eucharist in the church takes its meaning from the faith of the community in Jesus. Just as belief in him as a miracle worker never sufficed, so a water baptism will not suffice unless it takes its meaning from belief in Jesus as manifested by the presence of his Spirit. If people go to the font to be healed of their blindness, the font is Jesus himself and the healing results from faith.

The meaning of the eucharist depends upon a previous acceptance of Jesus as Wisdom. Only then can people "eat his flesh and drink his blood." Merely participating in the eucharistic ritual does not bring eternal life. Faith first and then the eucharist bring eternal life. People must never settle for ritual, for without faith the ritual becomes a lie.

Some in the early church may have already fallen into the temptation of emphasizing ritual over meaning, the danger of any organized religion. The gospel of John reminded those communities, as well as contemporary communities, to be careful not to lose the foundation: personal faith in the Lord. Then sacraments not only make sense but become indispensable.

Other Sacraments in the Fourth Gospel

Some also find references to other sacraments in this gospel: the eucharist in chapter 2 because of the reference to the wine or

matrimony; orders in chapter 17; and penance in chapter 20. Most
commentators see little or no foundation for the sacraments of the
eucharist, matrimony or orders in these texts. The commission to
forgive sins in chapter 20:

> Receive the Holy Spirit, if you forgive the sins of any, they
> are forgiven; if you retain the sins of any they are
> retained (20:22)

is given to the disciples, to the church and may well reflect the common practice. Some see a similar reference here to those found in
Matthew 16:19 and 18:18, in which first Peter and then the whole
church are given authority to forgive sins. The church of the
Beloved Disciple forgives all sins since Jesus also forgave the great
sin of apostasy by his disciples and wished them only peace. He
returned to them as risen Lord after they had abandoned him, and
twice he wished them peace (20:19, 21). In the context of human
failure and great sin the church wishes its members only peace, following the example of the Lord.

Suggestions for Reflection

1. The position of eucharistic teaching in chapter 6 is unusual.
   Does the explanation help in understanding the eucharist?
2. Some see the foot washing as eucharistic. How can the foot washing relate to the eucharist?
3. Is Wisdom necessary for the celebration of the eucharist?
4. Worship in spirit and truth is the touchstone of worship in this
   gospel. How does this apply today?
5. Do the eucharistic overtones in the multiplication of the loaves
   give any insights into eucharistic overtones in any celebration of
   an ordinary meal?
6. Does the eucharistic teaching in chapter 6 mean that no one can
   be saved unless he or she celebrates the eucharist?
7. The theme of rebirth in the Spirit in chapter 3 is a broader concept than that of the sacrament of baptism. How does this affect
   your understanding of the sacrament? Is rebirth the same as
   baptism in the Spirit as understood in the Charismatic Movement?

8. Do you see any references to baptism in chapter 9? Why would the author relate the water to Jesus?

9. Are the other references to water in the gospel clearly baptismal? What are some other possibilities?

10. Is this gospel sacramental in a broad sense rather than sacramental with reference to the official sacraments of the church?

11. How do the sacramental concepts in this gospel relate to the church's present teachings about the sacraments?

6.

The Farewell Discourses

Chapters 13 to 17 are frequently called the farewell discourses. Discourses, plural, because one seems to end with "Come then, let us be on our way" (14:31), only to be followed by the parable of the Vine and the Branches and two additional chapters. Then, at the beginning of chapter 17, the author states: "After he had spoken these words, Jesus looked up to heaven and said..." (17:1).

In these chapters the author moves from Jesus speaking to everyone to Jesus speaking only to his own. The final person who does not belong, Judas, leaves in 13:30. The process of separation is complete. The remnant remains, and Jesus speaks of the fullness of revelation completed only on the cross.

■   **The Command of Love**   ■

In the first of these discourses Jesus gives the new love commandment, so important in this gospel, and clarifies the measure by which love will characterize this community:

> A new commandment I give you. Love one another as I have loved you, so you also should love one another (13:34).

"As I have loved you" differentiates this command from any other commandment of love. Jesus, the Good Shepherd, would give his life for the sheep. That measure would characterize the Christian community. Not content with the "love your neighbor as yourself" of the synoptics, this gospel pushes the love command to its utmost: love to the point of being willing to die for the brethren.

■ The Holy Spirit, the Paraclete ■

Also in these chapters the author introduces the Paraclete, the Holy Spirit.

> And I will ask the Father and he will give you another Paraclete, to be with you always, the Spirit of truth which the world cannot accept because it neither sees nor knows it (14:16–17).

> The Paraclete, the Holy Spirit, that the Father will send in my name, he will teach you everything and remind you of all that I have told you (14:26).

> When the Paraclete comes whom I will send you from the Father, the Spirit of truth that proceeds from the Father, he will testify to me (15:26).

> For if I do not go, the Paraclete will not come to you, but if I go I will send him to you. And when he comes he will convict the world of sin and righteousness and condemnation. Of sin because they do not believe in me; righteousness because I am going to the Father and you will no longer see me; condemnation because the world has been condemned. I have much more to tell you, but you cannot bear it now. But when he comes, the Spirit of Truth, he will guide you to all truth (16:7–13).

Functions of the Paraclete

The Holy Spirit, the advocate, the Paraclete will protect the disciples. He will teach and guide; he will bear witness to Jesus and enable the disciples to do likewise. With such a teacher the disciples will need no other teachers. The disciples will learn all truth from the presence of the Paraclete, the Holy Spirit.

Just as Jesus taught his disciples, and just as the disciples learned from the Beloved Disciple, so all was made possible by the presence of the one Spirit. In a world filled with confusion and complexity, the Spirit will guide all followers of Jesus. As Jesus himself taught and gave protection, so now the Paraclete sent from the Father and from Jesus will take on the responsibility of Jesus for his disciples.

From Father and Son

Unlike the other gospels the Fourth Gospel offers specific insights into both the nature and function of the Spirit. (R. Brown offers a detailed analysis of the Paraclete in an appendix of his commentary on the gospel, volume 2).

The Paraclete comes from and is related to both Father and Son:

He will come only if Jesus departs (16:7).

He comes from the Father (15:26).

The Father sends the Paraclete in response to Jesus' request (14:16).

The Paraclete is sent in the name of Jesus (14:26).

The Paraclete is also called the Spirit of truth (14:17; 15:26; 16:13).

He is synonymous with the Holy Spirit (14:26).

He is called "another Paraclete," implying that Jesus is also a Paraclete (14:16).

The Paraclete and the Disciples

The Paraclete also has a relationship to the disciples of Jesus as well as to the world:

The disciples will recognize him (14:17).

He is within and remains with them (14:16–17).

He teaches them (16:13).

He announces what will occur in the future (16:13).

He declares what belongs to Jesus and what does not (16:14).

He glorifies and witnesses to Jesus (15:26; 16:14).

He reminds the disciples of all Jesus said (14:26).

He speaks only what he hears, not of his own authority (16:13).

The Paraclete and the World

The world cannot see, recognize or accept the Paraclete (14:17).

The world rejects the Paraclete and in that rejection the Paraclete witnesses to Jesus (15:18–26).

The Paraclete proves the world is wrong, guilty of sin and to be condemned (16:8–11).

The presence of the Paraclete solves for this gospel the problem of the delay of the Parousia, the Second Coming of Jesus. Jesus has returned, for the Paraclete is Jesus present now in his community. Do not look for a future coming but look in the present for the presence of Jesus now in the community through the presence of the Spirit, the Paraclete.

The Paraclete and Future Generations

The Paraclete also solves the perplexing problem of preserving the revelation of God in Jesus for future generations. The Paraclete mediates *now* the revelation of Jesus to people of later generations. He does not teach new things but only what Jesus has taught. The Paraclete joins later generations of Christians to the ministry, death and resurrection of Jesus. Future generations of Christians can feel assured that what they believe goes back to the historical Jesus, for the Paraclete present in the church joins the present generation to those who listened and followed Jesus in the first generation of Christians.

■ The Prayer of Jesus ■

Please read John 17:1–26.
Chapter 17 forms the keystone for much of the theology of the Johannine community. This solemn chant by Jesus before he begins his final road to glory on Calvary explains much about how the Johannine community viewed the mission of Jesus. All culminates on Calvary, and here the disciples learn of the meaning of Calvary.
Jesus is still in this world:

Now, however, I come to you; I say all this while I am still in this world that they may share my joy completely (17:13).

As you have sent me into this world, so I have sent them into the world (17:18).

and yet he has already left:

I have given you glory on earth by finishing the work you gave me to do (17:4).

I am in the world no longer, but these are in the
world....As long as I was with them, I guarded them with
your name, which you gave me (17:11–12).

The author speaks as if Jesus already has entered into his final
glory and as if he is entering his final glory. Jesus is present and
absent at the same time. Jesus, who lived in this world but never
completely, expects the disciples to do likewise. They will be present
to this world and also absent.

■ Farewell Discourses in the Old Testament ■

This farewell of Jesus sounds similar to the farewell of the
patriarchs of the Old Testament. Jacob in Genesis 49 and Moses in
Deuteronomy 32 and 33 also gave their final thoughts and words to
their followers. Deuteronomy offers a parallel to the final testimony
of Jesus. In Deuteronomy 32 Moses turns away from the people and
addresses God in heaven, and in Deuteronomy 33 Moses blesses the
tribes for the future.

Here Jesus addresses God in heaven and prays for his followers, present and to come. For Jesus, however, the solemn prayer is
more than just a final testament, since it contains as well a sum-
mary of his mission and offers an impetus for his followers to follow
him in accomplishing this mission. Jesus offers his disciples not
only an impetus for their mission but assures them that he will
make their mission possible.

The Prayer and the Synoptics

Although none of these discourses appears in the Last Supper
scene of the synoptics, many of the themes spoken of here find a
counterpart in the other gospels.

Father, Lord of heaven and earth, to you I offer praise, for
what you have hidden from the learned and the clever
you have revealed to the merest children. Father, it is
true. You have graciously willed it so. Everything has
been given to me by my Father; no one knows the Son but
the Father, and no one knows the Father but the Son and
anyone to whom the Son wishes to reveal him (Matt
11:25–27; see also Lk 10:21–23).

The prayer also has a parallel to the Lord's Prayer of the synoptics with its petition, "May your name be holy." And the petition "deliver us from the evil one" has its parallel in "that you should keep them from the evil one" (Jn 17:15).

The author of this gospel presents in this chapter a long prayer by Jesus unknown to the other gospels but not completely out of character with what Jesus spoke in his ministry. The evangelist appears to offer a homily using the thoughts of Jesus clothed in the words of the preacher or evangelist. Jesus speaks thoughts similar to those the synoptics recorded but in the distinct style of this evangelist or, perhaps, of the one who inspired this gospel. The discourse should not be seen as a completely historical and a literal presentation, but neither should it be viewed as completely created by the author. The discourses are related to the Passover Supper, which contained long liturgical prayers, and surely Jesus would have modified these prayers, making them his own. The references to the hour, the treason of Judas, the mission of the disciples and his death—all are part of the historical situation of the Last Supper. But in this gospel the prayer of chapter 17 transcends the historical situation. Jesus has passed into eternity, made present now in the supper and then in the Johannine church. Actually, the prayer has become the prayer of the Johannine community with Jesus.

■ The Prayer and the Eucharist ■

Some of the Greek Fathers, Cyril of Alexandria and John Chrysostom, for example, relate this chapter to the eucharist. The *Didache* also contains some themes present here: the holy name is mentioned as also a petition that God will deliver the church from evil and gather it together in holiness. But the *Didache* also explicitly refers to bread and wine. This gospel makes no mention of the eucharistic elements. Later Christians saw in this chapter the eucharist, but, as already discussed, the author of this gospel places his eucharistic teaching in chapter 6.

■ The High Priestly Prayer ■

In the sixteen century the Lutheran theologian David Chytraeus (1531–1600) titled this chapter "The High Priestly Prayer." Since then many have accepted this as a prayer associated with Jesus as a priest and his apostles as the first Christian priests after

Jesus. In reality, the chapter contains a consecration but it is of Jesus and *all* his followers, not just the leaders of the Christian church. Chapter 17 may well be called the priestly prayer but the priestly prayer of all Christians. Jesus made himself holy so that all might be holy (17:19).

Divisions

Many offer divisions for this chapter—from three to seven— with various theories supporting the structure chosen. Four seems sufficient and in accord with the general ideas that are found within these divisions.

All Is Consummated (verses 1–8)
Jesus lifts his eyes to heaven. The twofold level in this gospel, heaven and earth, are joined because the earth now shows the glory of God. The hour of glorification on earth has come. Both God and the Son will be glorified. All will see both the power and goodness of God. Jesus came to give eternal life, and now, in the presence of death, all who believe and look upon the crucified Savior will experience life. Jesus has revealed God. People have known God through Jesus. Believers have come to see the compassion, kindness, mercy and fidelity of God in the ministry of Jesus. And they will see these same virtues in the death of Jesus. They will know Father and Son present in human life and in human death, and they will experience eternal life.

Jesus has revealed the name of God to his followers. In Exodus Moses wanted to know the name of God (Ex 3:13). God replies by not telling the name but assuring Moses that God will be present to him and to the people of Israel. God says: "I will be what I will be" (Ex 3:14) or "You will know who I am in your history," for the God of Moses is the God of Abraham, Isaac and Jacob, of Sarah, Rebecca, Rachel and Lea. Sometimes this dialogue with God and Moses uses the expression "I am" to translate into English the sacred name of God. This same expression becomes part of the Johannine tradition of titles of Jesus. The difference, however, clarifies the meaning of this effort to "name" God. The author of this gospel is not interested in some philosophical abstraction in naming God. Jesus now reflects this one God of Israel in his living and in his dying. To know God's name is to know God. To know God is to know Jesus, whom God has sent. Jesus bears the name of God, and his followers now know God through Jesus.

Jesus continues the revelation of Israel, for in Jesus God shows the divine qualities associated with the covenant of Moses. Jesus says that God is like a kind and loving parent anxious to respond to the needs of people. God is Father. The glory proclaimed in the prologue has been manifested in the ministry of Jesus and now culminates in the death of Jesus, in which all who gather around the cross will recognize the presence of God in every aspect of human life, even in dying.

Prays for All Confided to Him (verses 9–19)

Jesus prays for his disciples in relationship to their mission. They too will reflect the glory of God. Their commitment to the gospel of Jesus will manifest the same qualities that Jesus showed in his life: compassion, kindness, mercy and fidelity. They manifest the glory of God and in turn are caught up in this same glory.

Jesus will leave them but will never leave them. They need help. As God alone is holy, so Jesus wishes his disciples to be close to God, to be like God, to be holy, to be members of the household of saints in the one holy family of God. God the holy one will guard them for their mission since they are all united: God the Father, the Son, and the disciples. Those who only pretended to be so united have left, for they never really belonged (1 Jn 2:19). The ones who remain, the ones united with God and Jesus, must be full of courage and optimism because Jesus has made them to share in this joy with God his Father. They will accomplish their mission, for they continue the mission established by God alone.

The disciples must live in a real world and not in some "ivory tower" watching what unrolls before them. They will experience conflict, but the Word of God conquers all. The Christian life takes its source from the Word and then personifies the Word in the world in which believers live.

■ Holiness ■

Jesus makes all possible, for he has made himself holy so that his followers may be holy. "To make holy" or "to consecrate" means to set apart for a special task. Jeremiah was made holy (Jer 1:5), set apart for service to God and to people, before he was born. Moses consecrated the sons of Aaron to serve in the official priesthood of Israel. Once set apart the holy ones are given the necessary gifts to accomplish the service.

Jesus has separated himself from all that is foreign to God so that those who believe in him may also be separated from all that does not belong to God. When individuals accept Jesus as revealing God in life and in death, they become united to God through Jesus. They are holy and give glory to God by their lives in this world.

To make holy in truth; here "truth" denotes the divine reality and revelation. The Word of God reveals to humanity the true possibility of human life. Truth is the Word of revelation that has taken place in Jesus. The revelation by Jesus in living and in dying reveals God and humanity and joins them irrevocably.

Jesus offers himself in life and in death manifesting the divine qualities. Jesus glorifies God. To be made holy in truth means to accept Jesus as the revelation of God not in any abstract sense but in the fullest meaning of God entering into human life. Jesus revealed God as compassionate, as kind, as merciful and as faithful. Jesus revealed God as a kind and loving Father. This same God is never distant from the human family. God never abandons anyone. People can count on the presence of God in living and in dying. Jesus made this evident in his life and in his death.

Prayer for the Church at All Times (verses 20–23)
The unity of the church community reflects the unity of God the Father and the Son. Knowledge brings unity, and the Father knows the Son and the Son knows the Father. But more important, love makes the unity stronger. The Father loves the Son, and the Son loves the Father. God as Father and Son and all the disciples of the Son are united. Then the mutual love of the brethren reflects this divine and human unity. By being united in love, they will conquer the world.

■ Unity ■

These verses have been used frequently for ecumenical purposes referring to the unity of the Christian church. Depending on ecclesial positions, the verses can be used for an organic unity or a unity with differences. In fact, the verses have little to do with church unity. The primary unity is the unity with God accomplished through unity with Jesus. A mystical or spiritual unity results from the faith commitment to Jesus, which is made possible by God who draws people to Jesus, who in turn invites his followers into a unity with the divine community. The necessary outflowing of the unity with God through Jesus includes the unity accomplished by the love of the brethren. Unity already exists for those who have accepted

Jesus. The unity becomes humanly visible in the mutual love of the brethren.

Perhaps the author was conscious in these verses of some of the problems associated with the developing church. The common faith in Jesus should have brought a unity in life and in love, but often the early church suffered from the influence of evil and sin, which always mars faith, unity and love. With the vertical unity in place with God through Jesus, the horizonal unity in love is always possible.

■   Final Glorification   ■

Final Glorification (verses 24–26)

Jesus appeals to God his Father. He resolves that all his disciples will be with him and with God. They will see the glory of God more powerfully than Moses or the people of Israel saw the glory of God in the Exodus. God's glory belongs to God and to Jesus and to his followers. Where there is the one, there are the others. The final glorification of Jesus includes his disciples, bound eternally with God through the power of love.

The three predictions of the passion in this gospel—Moses and serpent (3:14); the Son of Man and "I am" (8:28); and the drawing of all to oneness (12:32)—are joined here at the Last Supper as well as on Calvary. All are united with God for Jesus is God's human face. When his disciples saw Jesus, they recognized the presence of God, who offers eternal salvation and eternal life.

The consecration of Jesus for the sake of his disciples forms the foundation for the Johannine mission. Only when they are holy can they bring others to holiness, and Jesus has made them holy. God has already blessed this community. They will live in love for each other, and by so doing, they will manifest the glory of God. They have to live in the world but as followers of Jesus they will bring a richness to that living that will overcome the evil and darkness. Jesus has so deemed. Chapter 17 helps explain the entire Gospel According to John, for it helps to explain the mission of Jesus and the mission of his followers.

Suggestions for Reflection

1. Jesus speaks only to his own in these chapters. Why is this important?

2. Judas leaves. What are your thoughts on Judas?

3. The Holy Spirit is like a counselor or defense attorney. How do you think of the Holy Spirit?

4. Jesus makes himself holy. Why is this the heart of the gospel?

5. Unity demands working for unity. How can the church work for the unity of all its members?

6. All share in the glory of God. How do people share in this glory?

7. Why should this prayer be the prayer of all Christians?

8. How can a Christian be in the world but not of the world? Does this make sense?

7.

The Passion of the Lord in the Fourth Gospel

---

*T*he title for this chapter might seem misleading. When people think of the passion of the Lord, they usually think of the painful experience that Jesus endured from the agony in the garden through the actual crucifixion and death. The synoptics display, at times in a graphic way, the suffering of the Lord as he faced his death. But in the gospel of John Jesus does not suffer. The road to Calvary is a glorious parade leading to the final hour of glory when he dies having fulfilled all that was expected of him. Then he communicates, hands over, his Spirit on the Beloved Disciple and upon his mother.

■ Paul and the Synoptics ■

Paul sees the death of Jesus in relationship to sin. Jesus has entered into human history, a tale of sinfulness and rejection of God. By his passion and death Jesus overcomes sin and reconciles humanity to God.

> I handed on to you what I myself received, that Christ died for our sins in accord with the scriptures (1 Cor 15:3).

> Jesus was handed over to death for our sins and raised up for our justification (Rom 4:25).

The synoptic gospels also see redemption in the expiatory death of Jesus. Jesus suffers a painful agony; he is mistreated and crucified for the remission of sins and the salvation of the world.

For the Son of Man came not to be served but to serve and
to give his life as a ransom for many (Mk 10:45).

■   **The Death of Jesus in the Fourth Gospel**   ■

But in this gospel Jesus accomplished redemption and the
experience of salvation in the incarnation and in the revelation of
God in his ministry. The passion and death are the return to glory.
Some texts, however, seem to maintain the twofold approach to the
death of Jesus. Jesus is the lamb of God who takes away the sins of
the world (1:29). Here the evangelist may have in mind Isaiah
53:5–7, in which the prophet speaks of the sufferings of the just servant of God.

God so loved the world that he gave his only son that
whoever believes in him may not die but may have eternal life (3:16).

In this verse the evangelist may be thinking of the sacrifice of Isaac
in Genesis 22. In the tenth chapter the shepherd gives his life for
the sheep (10:15) and in 11:50 Caiphas refers to the death of Jesus
for the sake of the nation.
In spite of these many references to the sacrificial death of
Jesus, the Fourth Gospel maintains its emphasis on the coming of
Jesus as Incarnate Word and Wisdom, offering salvation to all who
believe. Ultimately, however, the belief involves seeing in the death
of Jesus the glory of God.

■   **The Passion of Jesus in the Four Gospels**   ■

In the passion account the gospel of John comes closest to the
accounts of the final days of Jesus found in the synoptics The passion, death and resurrection of Jesus are the moments of the life of
Jesus that were quickly established in the church's tradition. This
does not mean, however, that each evangelist presents them in the
same manner. Most scholars see no literary dependence between
the Fourth Gospel and any of the synoptics. Some events appear
only in the synoptics.

The Passion Events Found Only in the Synoptics

Agony in the garden
Kiss of Judas
Flight of the disciples
Process before the Sanhedrin
Derision of Jesus as a prophet
Simon of Cyrene helps Jesus carry the cross
Lament of the women on the way to Calvary (Lk)
Initial offering of mixed wine (Mk, Mt)
Jesus' prayer for forgiveness of executioners (Lk)
Repentance of the good thief (Lk)
Derision of Jesus on the cross
Darkness
Cry of the dying Jesus: "My God my God,...(Mk, Mt)
Suggestion that he seek deliverance by Elijah (Mk, Mt)
Wrapping of the body
Women at the tomb
Purchase of spices (Lk)

Many of these can quickly be eliminated from the theology of the Fourth Gospel precisely because of the author's emphasis on the divinity of Jesus, the all-knowing Savior who determines his own destiny. As one who is divine, he will not suffer or be treated in an unseemly manner.

**The Passion Events Found Only in the
Gospel of John**

"Ego eimi," "I am"
Interrogation before Annas
First altercation between Pilate and the Jews
Private interrogation in praetorium
"Behold the man," "Behold your king"
Refusal to change title on cross
"Woman, behold your son..."
"I thirst"
"It is finished"
Piercing of Jesus' side
Nicodemus and ministrations

The synoptics view the death of Jesus as the end, a painful and sorrowful end. The author of this gospel sees the crucifixion in light of the glorification of the Lord. The passion and death are anticipations and signs of his final glorification since on the cross believers see the results of the work of salvation (12:32; 13:1). The passion of Jesus is triumph. Glory colors the atmosphere. The cross is the throne of the kingdom from which the powerful Savior reigns and from which he will communicate his Spirit.

■ The Passion in the Fourth Gospel ■

Please read John 18.

The chapter begins with Jesus in the garden, but unlike the synoptic gospels, he does not pray to the Father asking to be released from this hour. Jesus never suffers but is in complete control of the situation. His captors, along with the betrayer, enter the garden to apprehend him, but Jesus commands the situation. Jesus confronts the powers of darkness. Judas and the soldiers come out of the night and meet the powerful Lord Jesus, who answers their question. And immediately they fall to the ground.

Pilate

When Jesus meets Pilate the nature of his kingship becomes evident: Jesus is king by bearing witness to the truth, this same truth that makes all free (8:32). God is present in Jesus freeing people from the power of darkness and inviting them to come to the light and be free. Pilate appears in this chapter as basically a good, if weak, man. He asks Jesus, "What is truth?" (18:38). Secular power functions indifferent to the truth and freedom that Jesus offers. Faith alone is the response to the truth that Jesus offers, and Pilate cannot offer that response.

■ The Crucifixion ■

Please read John 19:1–42.

Unlike the Jesus of the synoptics, who needs assistance in bearing his cross, Jesus in this gospel bears the cross alone. The parade has begun that will lead to the glorification in his death. The chief participant will control his own destiny and fulfill what is expected of him.

The Faithful Ones on Calvary

At the base of the cross are the two most faithful followers: his mother and the Beloved Disciple. They hear his final testimony and accept the Spirit that he communicates to them. Both believe in him and in his ministry, and now both stand faithful to the end. Fittingly, they are first to receive the promised gift of the Spirit. Aware that he has accomplished all that was expected of him, he announces that "it is finished" and, bowing his head, hands over his Spirit to those present to receive it.

The Theme of Exaltation

The synoptics have predictions of the passion of the Lord during his ministry with the idea that it was necessary for Jesus to suffer and die (Mk 8:31; 9:31; 10:33–34 and parallels). This evangelist says it is necessary and fitting for Jesus not to die but to be exalted and glorified. The word *crucify* is found only in the narration of the facts. What looks like an terrible death in fact is the path to glory.

The word *exaltation* is related to Isaiah 52:13: the servant shall be exalted and raised up very high. The same idea is found in Acts 2:33 and 5:31, but for Luke it refers to the ascension after death. In the gospel of John the word is used not in relationship to an ascension after death but to an exaltation in death.

> And just as Moses lifted up the serpent in the desert, so must the Son of Man be lifted up, so that everyone who believes in him may have eternal life (3:14–15).

> So Moses made a bronze serpent, and set it on a pole; and if a serpent bit any man, he would look on the bronze serpent and live (Nm 21:9).

The verse refers to the cross, which indicates the necessity of faith to recognize this strange death as an exaltation. Eternal life results as a gift to those who will respond in faith.

John 8:28

> When you lift up the Son of Man, then you will realize that I am *(ego eimi)* and that I do nothing on my own but I say only what the Father taught me.

This prediction connects the exaltation with the Son of Man. The formula is both biblical and prophetic, expressing a twofold effect: the description of the action of God bringing either salvation or punishment. Jesus manifests God to the people, and they must be respond in faith. The cross reveals the choice offered: to believe in Jesus or to refuse to believe. The raising up, the exaltation, reveals Jesus as God present *(ego eimi),* humanly calling for a response.

John 12:32–33

> And when I am lifted up from the earth, I will draw everyone to myself. He said this to indicate the kind of death he would die.

This verse finds a counterpart in Jeremiah 31:8:

> Behold I will bring them from the north country, and gather them from the farthest parts of the earth.

Jeremiah refers to the restoration of the messianic people. The evangelist likes the theme of gathering together since all who believe are united by faith and love. Around the cross gather all those who believe in Jesus and who recognize the presence of God in him both in his living and in his dying.

■ Jesus Reigns from the Cross ■

Jesus, exalted on the cross, with the title of king over his head, shows regality. He overcomes the prince of this world and its darkness. God the Father has established in Jesus a force that will draw people together. In faith they will gather around the cross as the messianic congregation predicted and hoped for by the Old Testament prophets.

On the cross the gifts of salvation become evident in the exercise of the regal power of Jesus. People of faith are persuaded and freely attracted to come to the cross, see its meaning and experience the saving presence of God in Jesus, which will give them a value and purpose in life. The exaltation draws people of faith.

The passion of Jesus should not be viewed as negative. Nor should suffering be seen as always negative. Faith in a crucified Savior unites people. God is present in all aspects of human life, even in a cruel and lonely death.

The Hour of Jesus

Usually in the gospels the "hour" of Jesus is an eschatological theme designating the time of salvation, but even in the synoptic gospel it sometimes refers to the passion of Jesus (Mk 14:41). In the gospel of John the word takes on special meaning.

General Meaning

Please read John 4:21–23; 5:25; 16:25.
In these passages the meaning is broad and can be seen in the more general and eschatological sense. Jesus tells the Samaritan woman that the future eschatological hour has already come. This conveys something of the understanding of the eschatology in this gospel. The future is *now*. The same idea is present when Jesus refers to the dead hearing the voice of the Son of God, and the eschatological hour when Jesus will speak plainly of the Father. While these ideas have a broad meaning in the gospel, the more specific meaning refers to the passion and, in particular, the crucifixion of the Lord.

The Final Hour of Glorification

Please read John 2:4; 7:30; 8:20; 12:23–27; 13:1; 17:1.
Each of these instances refers to the final hour, the hour of glorification on the cross. At Cana the time for true wine is his passion and exaltation. Later, his enemies could not arrest him since it was not the time for the passion (7:30; 8:20). Chapter 12 shows some reminiscences of the agony in the garden, since Jesus is troubled. The hour has come for him to be glorified. Jesus will battle with the forces of darkness and will conquer, but the passion is always joined to the glorification that will accompany it.

The opening verse of the farewell discourses (13:1) introduces the final testament of Jesus. The author makes no distinction among the passion, death and resurrection. All are united as one hour of triumph, and in John 17:1 the hour introduces the solemn priestly prayer of Jesus. The prayer of the hour is a prayer of glorification.

The hour of the passion is not just an hour of the life of Jesus but the final and eschatological hour of salvation that Jesus fulfills as messiah. This hour cannot be easily divided into episodes, as in the synoptics, especially in Luke, but must be seen as the consummation of the meaning of the incarnation. As the gospel unfolds, so does the understanding of the hour. At Cana the "hour" is indeterminate, but in chapter 7 the "hour" clearly refers to the death. In the twelfth chapter the author attaches the additional theme of glory to the "hour," and in the final two references (13:1; 17:1) all notion of death is gone, with only the theme of glorification remaining.

By speaking of the hour of Jesus, the evangelist continued the basic eschatological stance of anticipating future events. All is fulfilled and completed as Jesus reigns as king from the cross on Calvary. People of faith gather around the cross and recognize the presence of God. In dying Jesus shows God's love and fidelity. God will be present to all people both in life and in death.

Mode of Jesus' Acting

Historically, Christians often interpreted the passion psychologically and physiologically. The psychological agony in the garden precedes the burdensome way of the cross as does the brutal treatment in the crowning with thorns and the scourging at the pillar. The Fourth Gospel treats the passion theologically and soteriologically, as a way to salvation.

Jesus Knows All

From the outset Jesus knows all that will befall him; he is "aware of all that would happen to him" (18:4). Just as Jesus alone knew the Father, so he alone knew his hour (13:1; 18:4) Jesus accomplishes all in full awareness of what should be done:

> After that, Jesus realizing that everything was now finished, said to fulfill the scripture, "I am thirsty" (19:28).

Jesus of the passion in this gospel is far from a passive victim or a reluctant captive. With full awareness of all of the events and their meaning for himself and for others, he controls what happens to him and brings them to the fulfillment expected of him in full liberty.

Serenity

In this gospel Jesus acts with serenity. With full dignity he commands the soldiers in the garden; with a similar attitude he responds to Annas and remains a king in the presence of Pilate. The way of the cross is not a defeat but a triumph. The cross becomes the throne from which the king will reign. No sorrow, no suffering will mar the power and dignity of the only Son of God.

Christian theology often views the cross as expiatory, a sacrifice for sins. The Fourth Gospel sees the crucifixion as the presence of salvation and the full revelation of the meaning of Jesus. The goodness of God overwhelms from the cross, for God has so loved the world to overcome all sins on the cross. The sign of this goodness finds expression in the gift of Jesus as God's Son, even unto death. Jesus dies, but his death is more than what seems apparent. In truth Jesus reigns in his death, for then he can communicate his Spirit to those who will receive it, and what better examples of such faith than his mother and the Beloved Disciple. The passion according to John ends in triumph, just as it began.

Suggestions for Reflection

1. Why did Jesus die, and why did he have to die such a cruel death?

2. Do you prefer the passion according to John, with its distinctive approach, or the synoptic versions? What makes them so different, and what is their special value?

3. The gospel of John is read on Good Friday. How does this affect your understanding of that celebration?

4. Why is the crucifixion the hour of glorification? Is this reading too much theology into the death of Jesus?

5. Jesus knows all and is always in control. How does this affect your understanding of the humanity of Jesus?

6. Jesus is king in his passion. In what sense can he be a king in his ministry and in the present church?

7. The people cried, "Crucify him!" Does this mean that Christians ought to blame the Jews for the death of Jesus?

8. When the Jews claim they have no king but Caesar, they repudiate their heritage because God was their king. Why would the author have wanted to emphasize this rejection of their heritage?

9. Jesus reigns from the cross and gives his Spirit. What role do the Beloved Disciple and his mother play in this scene?

8.

The Death of Jesus

The death of Jesus in the Fourth Gospel reveals the glory of God and also God as a loving parent, the Father of the beloved Son. Such statements may appear strange at first, but only through understanding this aspect of the theology of the Fourth Gospel can the reader fully appreciate both the christology and the anthropology of the author.

■ **Religious Experience** ■

Most religions and religious expressions have depicted God over and above human experience. The transcendent One, the "totally Other," has characterized many attempts for people to come to understand and relate to the "Ground of Being" or the Creator of all. To have a religious experience or moment usually has been depicted as uplifting, ennobling, an ecstacy that defies human ability to find adequate expression. But can God be found in the abject, the painful, the wrenching moment of death, especially a terrible death? Is God present only in the good moments of life and absent, or at least silent, in death, the great tragedy of life?

Of the many images of God in human history, some seem more suitable than others, even if some seem more prevalent. Creator or judge or lawgiver or all-knowing potentate quickly come to mind as examples as well as friend, father or mother. But which ones form a more adequate way of expressing the relationship that exists between God, the "totally Other," and people? Which human expressions and images better convey just how God exists within the sphere of human understanding?

Criteria of William James

William James has offered the classic analysis in his structuring of human religious experience containing clearly defined elements. When individuals or groups have an awareness of the divine, such moments remain unexplainable; they are ineffable. The individual is most often passive, and the experience is transient. But the one so touched learns something; a noetic content accompanies the religious moment. The usual examples of these moments in the life of an individual or a group are positive, even if they contain some frightening moments. But can these same elements be found in negative aspects of human life, even in dying?

■ The Death of Jesus in the Fourth Gospel ■

In depicting the death of Jesus the Fourth Gospel presents God not hiding behind pious platitudes nor abstract philosophical expressions but like a loving parent, a Father. The death of Jesus is also the glory of both God and Jesus.

■ The Revelation of God as Father ■

Certainly the Fourth Gospel presents Jesus revealing God in his ministry. "He who sees me, sees him who sent me" (12:45); "he who has seen me has seen the Father" (14:9). The religious experience of God in this gospel is equated with the actual seeing of Jesus of Nazareth. Jesus reveals God to people—precisely as a kind and loving parent, as a Father. This revelation also continues in the death of Jesus.

Throughout the gospel the author strives consistently to show how God can be a Father to the human family. This forms the basis for the religious experience. Perhaps nowhere is this revelation more evident than in the Son living and then dying according to the will of God, his Father (4:34; 17:4). Jesus offers his own life—no one takes it from him (10:17–18)—and in his words and signs people find themselves introduced into the very company of God precisely as a loving Father.

■ The Revelation in Jesus' Self-Offering ■

Jesus freely lays down his life, but always this offering remains the work of God the Father (3:17; 5:36; 10:18). The hands of

God, Father of Jesus, contain all (3:35). Salvation, though accomplished by Jesus in his free offering of himself, flows from God, who offers both the means and the way. Where the Father is, there is the Son, and vice versa (5:23; 11:4; 13:31). The Father loves the Son always (3:35; 5:20; 17:23) and gives testimony to him (5:31–32; 8:18). The Father also seeks the glory of the Son on earth (8:50), and in turn the Son seeks and manifests the glory of God his Father (12:28; 17:1). And, finally, the Father raises up the Son when he has completed his offering of himself on the cross.

Jesus Offers Himself

Jesus as Word Become Flesh and as Son, and as human, responds to God by offering himself to God, his Father. This self-offering reveals who God is to people (4:34; 6:38; 8:29). As the Son knows the Father (17:25), honors God (8:49), loves God (14:31) and seeks God's glory (7:18)—not his own glory (8:50)—so this same Son leads all to God as Father (6:44; 12:26; 14:6).

The historical intervention is summed up in 13:3, 8:14 and 16:28. Jesus accomplishes all in the form of an obedient offering of himself to God and to people. The gift made to humanity by God in the sending of the Word, the Son, means nothing unless offered again to God as Father. Jesus accomplished this in his ministry and especially when he reigns from the cross, offering salvation to all humanity, represented and symbolized by the presence of the two perfect disciples, his mother and the Beloved Disciple.

The Meaning of *Uper Nous* ("For You")

Uper nous ("for you") defines the life of Jesus (10:11, 15). Throughout his ministry Jesus acted for others. He offered himself as the lamb of God and thus took away the sins of humanity (1:29). The alienation that people had experienced previously in their relationship to God has been eliminated. Now all people can stand in the presence of God as daughters and sons, feeling comfortable in the presence of God as intimates knowing the love of God for all.

This offering finds its culmination in the cross, where Jesus reigns supreme. He remained faithful to God and faithful to people (13:1; 15:12). Jesus lived open to the presence of God and open to all people. His own religious experience became the gift he presented to others. On the cross the offering of Jesus as the Word and Son of

God makes the meaning of life more clear: people are to live fulfilling the will of God and remaining faithful to God and to humanity even to the point of death. In a rebellious world this stance of Jesus between heaven and earth manifests the proper position for all who seek a relationship with God.

■ The Testimony of the Word, the Son ■

The offering of the Son to the Father is not the only content of the revelation. Jesus offered his testimony in words and signs from the time the Word first appears in human history. The work of Jesus and his word find full expression in 17:4. The glory of God becomes intertwined with revealing the name of God as Father. Jesus tries to convey this one Word to people in many words and deeds. God is not just a creator or judge or lawgiver or some absent potentate. God is present as a kind and loving parent in all of human history, especially through the life, ministry and death of Jesus of Nazareth. The many words of Jesus both in preaching and in his signs become one Word: God is like a loving Father for all in every aspect of human life, including dying.

All of the acts of Jesus find relationship to this one Word (5:17–23). Jesus does not act alone but always with the Father. The Word as acted out shows more than just walking or talking or eating. Jesus gives life and shows in the ordinary aspects of living the presence of God. Moreover, all of his words and deeds find their fulfillment in his dying first and then in his resurrection. The religious experience in human life culminates in a resurrection from the dead, but not without the dying. Jesus lives forever, so all who accept the revelation will live forever, but this (5:21) will not exclude human death. The signs of Jesus that point to the love of God are also the acts of God the Father. They reveal God and humanity. Only those who can recognize the presence of the glory of God in the ordinary life of Jesus, including his death, accept the revelation.

Manifestation of Jesus and the Knowledge of God

In the ministry of Jesus he reveals who he is, and this includes his proper relationship with God as Father. Many refer to the Abba principle as the key to understanding the meaning of Jesus. The gospel of John more than the other three gospels demonstrates this close relationship between God and Jesus. He has seen all with God his Father (8:26), and what he reveals is precisely God as Father.

The object of the revelation is Jesus and God (8:14; 10:25). He not only reveals God but testifies to God. The one revelation is both Jesus as human and God as Father. In the Fourth Gospel Jesus speaks of himself as life and light and judgment (6:35; 8:12; 10:14; 11:25; 14:6). In each of these the "I" is the attribute. The bread of life is Jesus; the light of the world is Jesus. Those who turn to the light, eat of the bread, find in Jesus not only his personal meaning but the revelation of the meaning of God.

Jesus expresses in his life the Word Become Flesh. In his offering in both ministry and death he offers himself for all. The life offered he has received from God his Father as a gift. He then offered this life to people who accept him and believe. Through signs and words people came to believe in him as the revelation of God. The one revelation, the one Word, is God as Father, and in this world the revelation finds meaning in the living and especially in the dying of Jesus.

■ God Revealed in the Death of Jesus ■

The revelation of God as Father in the life of Jesus comforts people. But this gospel also claims that God is revealed in the actual death of Jesus. If God is primarily presented as Father in this gospel, how can a kind and loving parent be manifest in the death of Jesus?

The death of Jesus may be seen as an example of a cosmic battle between good and evil. In his death Jesus achieves a decisive victory over Satan. The author of this gospel clearly presents Jesus as triumphing over death. He rules from the cross; the cross is his throne. Because this is also a revelation of God, then the author must have some profound reason to offer a revelation of God as Father in the dying Jesus.

Throughout his passion Jesus rules. He knows all, controls all, permits all; he alone will lay down his life (10:17–18). The author also has Jesus scourged, after which Pilate proclaims: "Behold the man." ("Look at this abject and dehumanized individual. You Jews have nothing to fear from him, nor does Rome.") This same beaten and wounded person goes his own way to Calvary, carrying his own cross and then dies in full control of all.

God Present in Dying

For the author of this gospel God is present and offering himself not only in the heights of ecstacy but in the very depths of pain and suffering. The one who revealed God's human face in this gospel also showed God's face in his very dying, even in a painful and sorrowful death. God is not absent from any aspect of human life, especially the end of human life, when people often lie alone, forgotten and in pain. But why does this author insist on calling God a Father, and why is the death the most significant revelation?

Unlike the synoptics, salvation is accomplished in the Fourth Gospel through the Word, which is then fulfilled in the death of Jesus. Jesus gives his life for the sheep (10:11), and on the cross he gathers the dispersed people around himself (12:32). Jesus triumphs on Calvary with an atmosphere of glory, and then he reigns from the cross as his throne. His death is the end of a glorious parade, and in dying Jesus himself is exalted (3:14; 8:28; 12:32). Jesus has drawn all people to himself on his cross: Nicodemus, Joseph of Arimathaea, his mother, the Beloved Disciple and both Jews and Romans. In faith people are called to look upon the dying Jesus in an abject and humiliated mode and see the face of God. God is not absent from the most wretched of human conditions, including the terrible and painful death by crucifixion.

If God is present in this most sorrowful of all deaths, then God is present in all moments of life and death. In the actual dying of Jesus, in which he remains faithful to God his Father and faithful to people, those of faith can see the presence of that same God. The final revelation of God makes God present in every aspect of human life, and knowing God is present even in a terrible death, people experience salvation. Faith in a crucified Lord can unite people and enable people not only to live a life similar to that of Jesus but to die knowing that God is not distant. Jesus revealed God's face in how he died. Rejection, misunderstanding, pain and suffering are never foreign to God's presence. The Word Become Flesh speaks eloquently in his reign from the cross, and those of faith gather around that cross and experience the saving presence of God in their own lives.

Religious experience involves not only the mountaintops of mysticism and ecstacy but also can be found in the dying of Jesus and in one's personal death. Faith finds its fullest fulfillment when the religious person can look upon a crucified Jesus and see the presence of God. The transient, passive, noetic and ineffable elements are all present around the cross of Jesus.

God is Father not only to Jesus but to all people. God remains with Jesus in his living and in his dying and, as a loving Father who is God, raises Jesus up. To preserve Jesus from dying would mean that God was not present in human death. To prevent Jesus from dying a painful death would imply that God is not present when people die in sorrow and pain. Surely that is the common death.

■   God as Father   ■

This theology, however, does not answer the other question: why God as Father? No one really thinks that God is male or female. God must be both and neither. The revelation of God as Father comes not only from an Ancient Near Eastern culture but also from the limitations placed upon the human revealing the divine. God could have become female in the same way God became male. However, Jesus as God's human face, the revelation of God, was a first-century Jewish male. Within that context and culture God became his Father, although Jesus also used images of God as a mother.

No human father is perfect, and so the imagery fails. The same would be true if God were spoken of as a mother. Christianity calls God Father after the example of Jesus, and to deny such appellation would be to deny the historicity of both Jesus and his tradition in the church. Perhaps contemporaries can find some resolution to the meaning of God as Father by thinking of the best qualities of a father and then add to them the best qualities of a mother and then recognize that God is something like that. Better, look at how Jesus lived and died and believe that in him, as the Fourth Gospel tells us, believers have seen God.

Suggestions for Reflection

1. Is religious experience common in people's lives?
2. How would you apply the principles of William James to Jesus in the Fourth Gospel?
3. Why is it easier to believe in God when things are going well?
4. If bad things happen to good people such as Jesus, how can God be good and loving?
5. Do most people die a peaceful and happy death?
6. Why does the Fourth Gospel place so much emphasis on the death of Jesus?
7. God is present even in a painful death. What is your reaction to this statement?

8. How would you relate the death of Jesus to your own death or the death of someone you love?

9. Is calling God a father helpful or not? Why do some women have problems with the image of God as a father?

10. Does the Fourth Gospel offer any help in understanding what God is like?

9.

The Resurrection Appearances

*T*he meaning of the resurrection of Jesus involves more than just a return to life. Resuscitation is not resurrection. With the resurrection Jesus enters into his final and definitive mode of existence. Now Jesus is Messiah in power, able to communicate his Spirit to others (Acts 2:36). Jesus has lived and died as the one faithful Son of the Most High and has transcended space and time. Now everything in this world, especially human beings, can be the means by which he can further communicate with his followers and with all people open to faith.

■ The Resurrection in the Synoptics ■

The synoptic gospels see the resurrection as the climax of Jesus' ministry. In Mark, although the original ending concludes with the women leaving the tomb bewildered (Mk 16:8), the longer ending includes material that gives the impetus for evangelization. The risen Lord changes everything. Matthew not only has an appearance to the women but concludes with a final and exultant commissioning of his apostles (Mt 28). Luke narrates the appearance to the disciples on the road to Emmaus and to the other disciples in Jerusalem (Lk 24). In each instance the experience of the risen Lord gives rise to Easter faith and Easter preaching.

■ Individuals and Places Associated ■ with the Resurrection

The four gospels do not agree concerning the various individuals and places associated with the resurrected Lord. Some have appearances in the area around Jerusalem (Luke, John and the

Marcan appendix, 16:9–20). Others have appearances in Galilee (Matthew and John and possibly the Marcan appendix). Jesus also appears to Mary Magdalene in John, Matthew and the Marcan appendix. In addition, Jesus appears to Peter in Luke and Paul, to two disciples in Luke and the Marcan appendix and to the eleven gathered together in Luke, John and the Marcan appendix.

The divergences may not necessarily connote a confusion of historicity; they could exemplify the events chosen by a particular faith community to suit its needs. An analysis of the various appearances in the gospels uncovers a common pattern: the followers are bereft of Jesus; he appears to them, greeting them and offering some encouragement by his very appearance; they ultimately recognize him, believe in him as resurrected and receive a mission. Not every appearance has all of these characteristics, but all fall within this general outline.

■ Resurrection Appearances in the Fourth Gospel ■

Please read John 20:1–31.

The gospel of John does not emphasize the resurrection. His interest centered on the glorification of Jesus in the crucifixion. Jesus reigned from the cross and was exalted, glorified and actually communicated his Spirit to those present in faith on Calvary, his mother and the Beloved Disciple. The resurrection expresses this new creation, which was accomplished in the crucifixion. Now Jesus can call his disciples brothers for the first time because now that they have received his Spirit—they too can call God their Father, as Jesus did.

■ Jesus and His Friends ■

The earlier chapters in this gospel contain numerous encounters between Jesus and individuals—from Nicodemus and the Samaritan woman to the man born blind to his closest followers. Not surprisingly, the final chapters treating the resurrection contain a number of encounters between Jesus and people of faith. An essential note to the resurrection appearances is the presence of Jesus to his friends when they are in need. In each instance after the resurrection the followers of Jesus experience some problem, including the lack of faith; his very presence is enough to resolve their dilemma as each becomes a believer.

The first two appearances are associated with the tomb: Simon Peter and the Beloved Disciple (20:1–10) and Mary Magdalene (20:11–18). The second pair of episodes in this chapter takes place with gathered disciples (20:19–29), concluding with the reaction of Thomas and his profession of faith.

Peter and the Beloved Disciple

The chapter begins with Mary going to the tomb. Unlike the synoptics, this gospel has Mary visiting the tomb twice. In her first visit she sees the tomb empty, concludes that the body had been stolen and runs to tell Simon and the Beloved Disciple. The evangelist paints delicately the relationship between these two disciples. Upon hearing the message from Mary they run to the tomb. The Beloved Disciple arrives first but allows Peter to enter first. Peter notes the carefully placed linen but the author makes no mention of Peter's reaction. The Beloved Disciple then enters and his reaction culminates the episode. He sees and believes (20:8).

Each responded differently to what he saw. Both surely saw the burial garments and the head piece without the body, but only the Beloved Disciple believed. In the Pauline list of appearances of the risen Lord, Jesus appears first to Simon (1 Cor 15:5), but the gospel of John knows of one who believed even before seeing, the Beloved Disciple.

The report of the garments laid carefully aside has many interpretations. Perhaps the best can be found within the gospel itself. Lazarus in chapter 11 comes forth from the tomb "bound with linen straps and his face wrapped in a cloth" (11:44) to be resuscitated and eventually to die again. Jesus leaves the burial clothes in the tomb, revealing to those of faith that Jesus, unlike Lazarus, has been raised to eternal life.

Mary Magdalene

Mary Magdalene's second visit to the tomb comes from a tradition independent from the tradition of the previous visit to the tomb by the two disciples. The evangelist first removes Simon and the Beloved Disciple from the scene (20:10) to allow for the very personal encounter between Jesus and Mary. The other gospels mention women going to the tomb on that first Easter morning. The gospel of John mentions only Mary. Apart from Peter, James, John and Judas, Mary Magdalene is the most frequently mentioned follower of Jesus in the gospels (fourteen times). The writer of the gospel also uses the literary device of having angels ask Mary some questions. This affords the possibility of another reaction as Mary comes to faith. Mary's first visit brings about a negative reaction, for she believes that the body has been stolen. Now the gospel continues this negative reaction, for she still believes that the body has been taken away on her second visit. Quickly, however, the negative tone gives way to the positive coming to faith. Jesus appears, but Mary does not recognize him. The theme of failing to recognize Jesus is present in other episodes in this gospel (21:4–7) and also in Luke (24:13–31). But when Jesus calls her by name, she immediately responds in faith. Just as the Good Shepherd knows his sheep by name and they respond to his voice, so the believer in Mary responds to the sound of the Master's voice as he calls her name. Mary's faith exemplifies all who belong to Jesus. "I know my sheep and mine know me" (10:14).

Once Mary recognizes him, Jesus instructs her not to continue to cling to him, but as in the case of the Samaritan woman, Jesus directs her to become a missionary to others. Mary will announce to the brothers of the Lord that he is risen. Jesus will eventually leave them all, but since he has been glorified on the cross, now his disciples must accept and continue to fulfill his mission. Mary accepts her responsibility to announce the risen Lord to his other followers.

Jesus also announces to Mary that he is ascending to his Father and her Father. The author here reiterates where Jesus truly belongs, whence he has never left (1:18). Mary believes, and now her home also is above even while she lives in this world. After her first visit to the tomb Mary told his disciples, "They took the Lord from the tomb" (20:2). Now she announces that she has seen the risen Lord (20:18).

The Distraught Disciples

Other gospels also narrate an appearance of the risen Lord to the apostles or the disciples (Lk 24:36–49; Mt 28:16–20 and the longer ending of Mk 16:14–18). The fourth evangelist has his own way of presenting the risen Lord to the disciples. The first reaction of the disciples was confusion and doubt at the reports of the risen Lord. Both Peter and the Beloved Disciple ran to the tomb but, as already noted, only the Beloved Disciple, who arrived first and waited for Peter, saw and believed (20:8). Jesus later mysteriously comes to the disciples in the upper room where they gathered "for fear of the Jews" (20:19). They had failed him and must have wondered what he would say when he saw them if he truly was risen. Jesus arrives in an unusual way and wishes them only peace, not a wish but a fact. At the Last Supper he had promised peace (14:27–28); now he offers it. Showing them his hands and his side removes all doubt regarding his identity. Their insight in recognizing the Lord brings them joy, for in recognizing him they have renewed their faith. In the midst of human failure and sin Jesus offers forgiveness and hope for a better future. Into this context the evangelist has placed the commission to the church to forgive sins.

Peace in Ancient Near Eastern tradition means the best of everything. Peace means a hope that the recipient will live to see his or her children's children, have fertile flocks and fields, be on good terms with family and neighbors and realize the goodness of God in life. Peace means everything. His disciples had failed, and Jesus wishes them peace, twice.

The power to forgive sins in this gospel is given to the whole community; the author stipulates that the "disciples" are gathered, not just the twelve. Forgiveness is not only a juridical process in this gospel but a proclamation of peace that looks to the future and a new existence. Peace will come when a person accepts his or her failure and relies on the mercy and forgiveness of God mediated through his church in Jesus. For the first time the gospel of John, in the context of the failure of the disciples to remain faithful to the Lord, refers to a forgiveness of sins as belonging to the church.

The disciples receive the Holy Spirit, as the Beloved Disciple and the mother of Jesus already had received on Calvary. Now they can represent Jesus to others and in the world. Just as in Genesis the breath of God brought into existence a human being in the image and likeness of God (Gn 1:26–27; 2:7), so now the breath of Jesus in giving the Holy Spirit to his disciples brings about human beings who are created in the image of the Son of God.

Thomas

Thomas, not present at the above appearance, is present a week later in a much troubled state. He doubts and wants to have the resurrection of the Lord "clinically" verified to his own satisfaction. Like the previous appearance to the other disciples, Jesus wishes them peace first and then deals with Thomas. Jesus invites him to examine his hands and side. Immediately Thomas becomes a believer. The disciple who doubted the most gives expression to a profound profession of faith: "My Lord and my God" (20:28); that is, you are Lord for me and you are God for me. If the gospel ended here the author would have offered four different reactions to the risen Lord. But the author or editor is not satisfied and adds yet another. The Beloved Disciple believed at the tomb; Mary Magdalene believed when Jesus called her by name; the disciples believed when they saw the risen Lord; and Thomas believed when the risen Lord challenged him to believe. The chapter ends, however, with the encomium: "Blessed are those who have not seen and yet believe" (20:29). Such are the followers of the Beloved Disciple in his community as well as followers throughout the ages.

Please read John 21:1–25.

The final chapter contains the appearance of Jesus to the disciples while fishing and the rehabilitation of Peter in the presence of the Beloved Disciple. Both individuals have already been studied. The material in this final chapter is Johannine, but some of it appears in the synoptic tradition (Lk 5:1–11; Mt 4:18–22). Now the disciples will become "fishers" of all people just as they had previously been fishermen in the sea of Galilee.

Scholars have long recognized this chapter as coming from a different hand than the previous chapters. Most likely the chapter deals with the founding of the church as well as a resurrection appearance. This appearance seems totally independent of chapter 20, for the disciples act as if they have never seen the risen Lord. Although all of the events in this chapter take place in one locale on one morning, the chapter can easily be divided into two parts, 21:1–14 and 21:15–24. The first concerns the disciples in general, and the second involves Jesus with Peter and the Beloved Disciple.

In the first episode the disciples are unsuccessful in their fishing (21:3). Continuing the theme of nonrecognition in this gospel, when Jesus appears on the shore they think he is a friendly stranger. In the synoptics Jesus calls his disciples while fishing and foretells that they will be fishers of men (Mk 1:16–20; Mt 4:18–22). Luke's version of the vocation scene emphasizes the abundance of fish (Lk 5:1–11). In the Fourth Gospel the miraculous and abundant catch brings about recognition of the risen Lord. Peter either clothes himself because naked or belts his garment to swim. The impetuous Peter reacts quickly, even though they are not far from shore. The more thoughtful Beloved Disciple remains in the boat while they row to shore. Following the theme of the previous chapter, the disciples are in need and the presence of the Lord brings belief.

The meal and the fish fill out the missionary symbolism. The precise number of fish has tantalized scholars for years. It could mean the total number of species of fish known to Greek zoologists, or the number could have Old Testament counterparts, or it is a magic number because the single integers cubed add up to the number 153. Whatever the possible meanings, fundamentally the abundance of fish shows how successful the followers of Jesus will be in fishing for their fellow human beings, for they will have the risen Lord with them.

The disciples eat and know the Lord in the context of the meal. Luke had a similar resurrection appearance in stressing the recognition of Jesus by the two disciples on the road to Emmaus (Lk 24:30, 42). Perhaps the followers of the Beloved Disciple reflected on the presence of the risen Lord as they continued to offer a eucharistic meal and so continued to eat with the risen Lord.

The final episode deals with Peter and the Beloved Disciple. Peter loves the Lord and will give testimony by giving his life for the sheep. The Beloved Disciple belongs with the Lord and he too will give testimony, not by death but by living and teaching; this witness continues in the gospel given the name John. And so the gospel ends:

> But there are many other things which Jesus did; were every one of them to be written, I suppose that the world itself could not contain the books that would be written (21:25).

Jesus was glorified on Calvary. Now he will be present to the church at all times, especially when his faithful ones are in need. The risen Lord, the faithful Son of God in death as in life, has completed his sojourn on earth. Having accomplished his mission as risen Lord he can fulfill his promise to be with his followers through the presence of the new Paraclete, the Spirit of truth who will guide them to all truth (16:13).

Suggestions for Reflection

1. Is Jesus really present to his friends when they are in need? Has this been your experience?

2. If the resurrection is not emphasized in this gospel, how is the theology of the risen Lord expressed in the gospel of John?

3. Jesus calls Mary by name. Why is this important in this gospel? How is this related to Jesus as the Good Shepherd?

4. Belief in the risen Lord characterizes chapter 20. What does it mean to believe in the risen Lord?

5. Mary became a missionary. The same was true for the Samaritan woman. Does this affect the role of women in the church today? Do you think women figured prominently in the Johannine community?

6. Peace and the forgiveness of sins are placed in a special context in this gospel. How does this affect your understanding of forgiveness? Does this power belong to the whole church or only to church leaders?

7. Peace is God's gift through Jesus in the midst of human failure and sin. How can the church express this?

8. Why would the author of this gospel have altered and expanded the material common in the synoptic gospels in chapters 20 and 21?

PART II

The Johannine Community and Theology

10.

The Eschatology of the Fourth Gospel

*U*sually the word *eschatology* connotes the last things: death, judgment, heaven, hell. The word comes from the Greek word *eschaton,* meaning "last" or "final." To talk about the eschatology of the Fourth Gospel and see the meaning in relation to the last things can cause some confusion because the gospel seems to take the future and bring it into the present. In one sense there are no last things in this gospel, for they have already been realized. Death, judgment and eternal life are all *now.*

■ **Future Eschatology** ■

Christianity arose with a belief that salvation for the human race lay in the future, but a very near future. Judaism encouraged among its followers a fervent hope for the imminent appearance of the messiah and for the wonderful age he would inaugurate. Since Christianity arose from Judaism, many of the early followers not only accepted Jesus as messiah but expected him to return in glory to fulfill the promise for the kingdom of God.

When Jesus returned not only individuals but all of humanity would be judged and experience salvation or damnation. With the delay of the Parousia, the Second Coming, eschatology became more individualistic. A person died, was judged based on the good deeds done while alive, and then experienced heaven or hell or, in the Roman Catholic tradition, purgatory while awaiting the general judgment of all.

■ **Present Eschatology** ■

Quickly, however, some of the early Christians came to believe that certain aspects of salvation and divine benevolence could be experienced in the present. Paul, for example in Romans 8:24, speaks of salvation as a present experience and as a future hope: "For we have been saved but only in hope."

With the delay of the Second Coming of Jesus and with the death of many of his closest followers, some Christians pushed the fullness of salvation into the distant future. But some of the early church communities, instead of focusing on the distant future, concentrated on the present reality. From this perspective the Fourth Gospel offers teaching on eschatology.

■ Salvation Is *NOW* ■

Throughout this gospel Jesus brings salvation, and in this offer of salvation an individual must decide to accept or experience judgment. Jesus promises and offers salvation and judgment here and now. The whole of Johannine theology is marked with this tendency. For Jesus, the hour of salvation has arrived, finally and irrevocably (4:23; 5:25). The eschatology is already realized; it belongs to the present, since the presence of Christ now dominates the thought of this gospel. The evangelist shifts the focus from the future to the present. Even when the Johannine Jesus talks about the future he focuses on the life of the community in the present with the presence of the Paraclete, the Spirit.

Future Eschatology in the Fourth Gospel

Please read John 3:18–19; 3:36; 5:21–29; 6:39–54; 9:39; 11:23–25; 12:25, 31, 48; 14:2–3, 18, 28.

A careful reading of the gospel, however, shows that some passages do refer to the future resurrection and judgment. The revelatory discourse in chapter 5 contains a reference to the raising of the dead (5:28–29); chapter 6 has four stereotyped sayings, "I will raise him up on the last day" (6:39, 40, 44, 54); and the same is found in John 12:48, though here it refers to judgment.

Some think that an editor added these references to the future to a gospel that had no references to a future eschatology. The editor wished to make this unusual gospel acceptable to the then-developing, more orthodox church with its teaching on future eschatology. The gospel, however, never seems to have circulated without references to a present and a future eschatology. To understand the teachings contained therein demands both. The real importance of these passages is whether the reference to future eschatology conflicts with the thinking of the evangelist. To try to assess this demands an understanding of the more general approach to eschatology in the gospel. Why does the evangelist emphasize the present more than the future?

■ Eternal Life ■

Please read John 3:15; 4:36; 5:39; 6:54–58; 10:28; 12:25; 17:1–4.

Salvation in the Fourth Gospel means eternal life, which the believer already has. The believer will pass through this world, the realm of darkness and death, to enter into the heavenly realm in order to share in the salvation of God. In this gospel God alone has life, and God gives it to the Son, who in turn offers it to others. The reversal of this process also takes place. People search for salvation, for life, and they find it through belief in Jesus. The author even offers a definition of eternal life: "Eternal life is this: to know you, the only true God, and him whom you have sent, Jesus Christ" (17:3). The mission God entrusted to Jesus the Son means eternal life for people. Eternal life or salvation, the goal of human existence, happens through the knowledge of God and Jesus Christ. Knowledge here should not be construed in a rational or theoretical sense. Knowledge means an inner acceptance and anticipation, and ultimately in the gospel of John, a communion between God and humanity.

Left alone no one can break out of the darkness that limits thinking and acting. Faith in the One who can open eyes to divine life fulfills a longing that all experience. Jesus does not postpone the promise of this life to some distant future. A life here and now on earth, this human life, becomes for the believer the transcendence of being. The one who accepts knows enduring security in the God who is the source of life. The believer also puts this life into action by living a life of love of the brethren. Resurrection has taken place for the believer, and he or she has a new self-understanding in relationship to God through faith in Jesus. When Mary states her belief that her brother Lazarus will rise on the last day, Jesus responds personally:

> I am the resurrection and the life; he who believes in me, though he die, shall live; whoever lives and believes in me shall never die (12:25–26).

Jesus teaches in this gospel that a faith relationship to him brings resurrection and life. Resurrection, like eternal life, is not some vague hope in something in the future but a present experience, for Jesus lives with his followers now. To live with faith in Jesus is already eternal life. This eternal life brings a quality of life that can never be destroyed even by physical death.

■ Judgment in the Present ■

Please read John 3:18–21; 5:22–30; 8:16–26.
The author also brings the contrasting concept of judgment into the present. Judgment still appears as divine judgment (8:50; 12:31), but now the Son judges as God previously had judged (5:22, 27). Human responsibility takes center stage. People must come to a decision to move from the darkness of sin and death to the light of faith and life. If people choose to remain in the darkness they have brought judgment upon themselves. If others choose to move to the light, they have already been judged; they have passed from darkness to light.

God ratifies what has already taken place on the human level. People bring this judgment upon themselves (3:11–21). When one decides against faith, then God has no other option than to ratify that personal choice. The word of Jesus, meant to be a word of salvation, becomes a word of judgment and condemnation. When people freely withdraw from God and choose to remain in sin and death they pass a death judgment upon themselves. No future judgment can be envisioned, for that has already taken place in human life (5:24). When a person ultimately dies, no final judgment takes place, only a fulfillment of a judgment brought on by his or her personal decision in life.

Usually Christians think of a personal judgment after death and a final judgment at the end of the world. Such thoughts find little foundation in this gospel. No one need wait for death or the end of the world to experience judgment. Moving from the darkness to the light of Jesus in faith accomplishes the judgment for everyone. People need not fear the future, for God fills up the future and has made the future present through faith in Jesus the Son.

■ Resurrection on the Last Day ■

Please read John 11:23–26.
The theology of this gospel acknowledges a future eschatology but then forces a rethinking of its meaning.

Jesus said to her, "Your brother will rise." Martha said to him, "I know he will rise in the resurrection on the last day." Jesus told her, "I am the resurrection" (11:23–25).

Martha introduces the expectation of the resurrection on the last day. Jesus gives another interpretation. Jesus himself is the resurrection and the life; here and now, in the presence of Jesus, resurrection actually takes place. In this very hour the dead are hearing the voice of the Son of God, and those who hear him in faith come to life and no longer die for all eternity. The teaching culminates when Lazarus himself comes forth from the tomb on hearing the word of Jesus. People may die physically, may lie in a tomb, but if they are people of faith, they live. They have heard the Word of God in Jesus, and they have responded. Physical death means nothing. The future has already begun for people of faith.

The Meaning of Johannine Eschatology

Discussions on the precise meaning of the present and future eschatology of the gospel of John continue. Some, as noted, dismiss all the references to the future as secondary additions; others see the need for a final completion of eschatology, begun in this life but brought to perfection in another. Instead of taking sides, perhaps the reader should accept the general outlook of the Fourth Gospel, which focuses on the present. The references to a future belong to the gospel as well, whether from the hand of the evangelist or another author, or from the thought of the inspirer of the gospel. Both are present in the gospel now, even if one is more prominent than the other. The future has already begun, although the future is also to be awaited.

The study of the passages involved does not dismiss the idea of a future but stresses, in relation to the sending of Jesus, the idea that he is come to save now and not to judge. Judgment remains but paradoxically Jesus does judge (5:30; 8:16). Only after an individual has chosen unbelief does the judgment become evident. A decision in the present in favor of belief or unbelief is itself the initial judgment. The author does not wish to enter into a polemic against judgment in the future as much as to emphasize the importance of salvation *now* because of the presence of Jesus in human history.

The same holds true for resurrection. In Jesus, the hope for fulfillment in resurrection has already taken place. The Christian belief in resurrection far surpasses all previous Jewish expectations. Jesus leads Martha (11:27) from her merely future-oriented hope to faith in the bringer of salvation and giver of life in the present. Martha becomes a model for all who turn from the incompleteness of the old religion to Christian faith, which alone brings true fulfillment.

Present and Future Eschatology

The evangelist probably has not deliberately rejected the primitive future eschatology of the church. He has, however, concentrated on the present. For this author, as for Paul, personal faith remains the crucial factor. Like Paul, the author of the Fourth Gospel describes Christian existence as life in faith, but without the eschatological tension between the already and the not yet that is characteristic of Paul. But does this involve only a shift in emphasis, or does the evangelist want to present a different theology?

■ Eschatology and the Individual Believer ■

The study of the individuals in this gospel has shown that the author is very much concerned with the fate of the individual believer. The individual confronts the meaning of existence and the possibility of salvation through faith. When speaking of salvation, the individual in this gospel stands out more prominently than in any other writing of the New Testament. This gives Johannine theology a certain existential flavor. In this approach interest inevitably shifts from the future of the world or of the human race or even the church as the community of faith, to the individual and his or her fate.

Entering through faith into the world of Jesus takes over the function of the Parousia as the completion of everything. This change in perspective, or perhaps personal attitude, can help explain the Johannine lack of interest in the future and the final things. For the evangelist, the coming of Jesus is itself the eschatological event. Christology does not function for eschatology; eschatology functions for christology. The fullness of salvation exists in Jesus (1:14, 16); Jesus offers this to humankind definitively and permanently (17:3); it is made accessible to all in faith (20:31). The decision made now brings about salvation and judgment and includes in itself the totality of the future.

Realized and Yet to Come

Perhaps even the disciples of the Beloved Disciple could not long maintain such a firm conviction about the reality of salvation and began to look to the future to confirm what had already happened, and so they spoke of the resurrection to life and the judgment on the evildoers (5:28–29). They accepted the reality of salvation present now but also needed a hope in a fulfillment of what had begun. They joined a realized eschatology to a future eschatology but never lost sight of the importance of the present.

■ The Future Assured ■

The eschatology of the Fourth Gospel teaches the need to contemplate the meaning of life and the search for personal existence. The future can be less important if all focus on the present reality, the fulfilled promise of salvation through faith. Wherever the history of humankind leads, or however an "end" may come, humankind can never again fall out of the love of God, who sent the only Son so that all might live through him for all eternity. The future is assured, since the future of the human race is God. Jesus has declared this definitively.

People of faith have died to darkness and sin. They have passed through judgment, and they experience eternal life because they know God and him whom God has sent. With such confidence in what has already happened the followers of Jesus face the present with a hope that has been fulfilled. God has spoken the Word in Jesus, and the Word brings salvation to all who respond in faith. For the believer, the future unfolds the reality already present. No one need fear for the good future for humanity. God has become part of human history already in Jesus. Live *now* in faith and the future will take care of itself.

Suggestions for Reflection

1. Does Jesus give life through his word? Is this eternal life? If judgment is already present, how would such a teaching affect the understanding of the sacrament of penance?

2. Does a realized eschatology respond to people's need? Why might it be important for the church today?

3. Can people lose a sense of the future with a realized eschatology?

How can both aspects of eschatology be harmonized? Would the gospel of John have wanted to have both types of eschatology accepted together? Why?

4. Does concern about death, judgment, heaven and hell give any insight into people's attitudes toward these experiences?

5. Why would people benefit from coming and living in the light of Jesus?

6. Does a realized eschatology affect your understanding of how people should live?

7. If eternal life is now, what does an afterlife mean?

8. Should Christians live their lives based upon the gospel even if no afterlife exists?

9. What makes you more comfortable: a realized eschatology or a future eschatology?

11.

The Community Behind the Fourth Gospel

*T*he Jesus tradition expressed in the gospels of Matthew, Mark and Luke differs from its expression in the gospel of John. Each evangelist responds to the needs of a particular community, and each offers an understanding of the ministry, life, death and resurrection of Jesus. The gospels do not come from isolated individuals but are part of a particular community's traditions; they express how the community lived the gospel of Jesus. The gospel according to John becomes intelligible only when readers realize that the gospel bears witness not just as the work of an individual, but as the work of an individual who founded, guided or lived within a specific community of believers.

■ The "Johannine School" ■

Today some people tend to talk about a "Johannine school." A group of early Christians lived as followers of a man called the Beloved Disciple. From this school Christianity has the legacy of the gospel of John and the letters of John. In the ancient world students tended to flock around a distinguished teacher and, through their research and teaching, continued the work of their master. Often enough these students would record the teachings of the master and prolong his effect through their writings. Something similar sometimes happens today. Law students, for example, might choose to study under a distinguished professor, and often enough the results of that study will find expression in legal briefs for generations. Whether a Johannine school ever existed or not, certainly an individual, the Beloved Disciple, did exist as a eyewitness to the Jesus tradition. He also had a profound influence on a group of early believers.

A Sectarian Community

The gospel shows a community that is narrow and sectarian. The members do not love the world:

> Do not love the world or the things in the world. If anyone loves the world, the love of the Father is not in him (1 Jn 2:15).

Jesus does not pray for the world (17:9) but rather prays that his followers may live in the world and not be part of it (17:14–16). Only those who recognize the voice of the Good Shepherd can follow him (10:3). Other sheep belong to the Shepherd, but they must learn to hear the voice of the Lord and join those who already belong (10:16). The sense of belonging to the community binds each individual to the Lord as it binds them to each other in love. If an individual chooses to leave the community, clearly he or she never belonged:

> They went out from us but they were not of us; for if they had been of us, they would have continued with us; but they went out that it might be plain that they all are not of us (1 Jn 2:19).

Even the great commandment of Love—"Love one another as I have loved you" (13:34)—seems sectarian. Unlike in the synoptic gospels the followers of the Lord in this gospel are not called to love their enemies. First and foremost, they must love the brethren, those who belong to the community. The author envisions a close-knit group of believers who emphasize the need for a commitment to the Lord and a profound love of the brethren that binds people together as one flock under one shepherd. That is enough.

Sect, Sectarian

Some people today do not like the word *sectarian* or *sect* applied to the Johannine community. The words have developed a negative connotation. Yet the original meaning of the word in English sheds light on this unusual community. It does not completely describe the community of the Beloved Disciple but can give some insights into this unusual church community at the end of the first century.

A *sect* is a body of persons distinguished by peculiarities of faith and practice from other bodies adhering to the same general belief system. The Johannine community was a sect within the larger

Christian church at the end of the first century. Its members shared the same general beliefs but separated themselves, or were separated, from other followers of the Lord through their interpretation of the Jesus tradition. As a community they chose to emphasize the essentials: faith and love. Only then would they permit other Christian practices to exist. They also seem to have welcomed disparate individuals and groups within their community with acceptance and not just tolerance. They were both sectarian and open to all.

A Diverse Community

Society in the Near East at the end of the first century offered something for everyone. Judaism was strong and varied; mystery religions with strange rituals attracted many with their promise of salvation. Early Gnosticism, the heresy that promised salvation through the communication of secret knowledge, had many adherents within both Judaism and even Christianity. Greek philosophy offered everything from the delight of Epicureanism to the rigidity of Stoicism. Commerce flourished with the ever-present Roman might.

Since no person can flee from societal influences but must pick and choose those which are helpful and avoid those which are harmful, the Johannine community had to learn to live in a diverse society and carve out its own sphere of influence. The community was composed of individuals, and many seem to have been quite strong in their individuality. Thus, many of the above influences would have been present in the community. Some people joined the community and later left, which further contributed to the sectarian nature of the group.

■   Groups Within the Community   ■

The gospel text gives evidence of several groups of people that formed part of the milieu of the Johannine community. Raymond Brown in *The Community of the Beloved Disciple* uncovers these various groups.

The first group was the opposition. Some individuals belonged to the "world," just as the members of the community did not belong to the "world." These people deliberately chose to stay in the darkness. They remained under the influence of Satan, the prince of darkness and the prince of this world. Their presence in the milieu would

have contributed to the feeling on the part of the Johannine community of being strangers in the midst of those who chose darkness.

A second group, associated with the former but distinct
because of tradition and opportunity, was the Jews. These Jews
never accepted Jesus and persecuted any Jew who professed belief
in Jesus. This group, sometime around the year 85, decided to
exclude from the synagogue anyone who acknowledged Jesus as
messiah. The Johannine Christian teaching that Jesus was one
with the Father, as well as their teaching that he had replaced the
Temple, and thus its sacrifice, directed a blow toward the heart of
Judaism that had to be resisted.

At this period some Jews also maintained a belief that John
the Baptizer, and not Jesus, was the messiah. The Johannine Christians reduced the importance of John; he was a witness to Jesus
who acknowledged that he had to decrease while Jesus increased.
Jesus alone is the true messiah, and John was his witness.

Still others were "crypto-Christians." They chose to remain in the
synagogue but privately believed in Jesus. They tried to live in both
camps. Eventually, especially with the decision of the Jews to include
in their prayers accusations against the followers of Jesus, these
crypto-Christians had to make a decision to profess publicly faith in
Jesus or to return to full participation in the faith of the synagogue.

The divergent views on christology uncover yet another group.
These Jewish Christians accepted Jesus only as a miracle worker
sent by God. They did not acknowledge the high christology advo-
cated in the gospel, accepting Jesus as God's special Son. For the
evangelist, these individuals could not be true believers even if they
could trace their acceptance of Jesus to the community in
Jerusalem. Initially people could accept Jesus as a miracle worker,
but such a faith had to develop into acceptance of Jesus as the eternal Son of God. The community had its share of low-christologists
and high-christologists.

The final group that appeared within the Johannine tradition
were Christians of other apostolic churches. These believers traced
their origin to Peter and the other apostles. They had developed a
moderately high christology emphasizing the origin of Jesus as the
miraculous intervention of God in human history through a virginal
conception, but without explaining his precise relationship to God.
Their ecclesiology also differed from the Johannine approach. Too
often, for the Johannine community, they were preoccupied with
corollaries to Christianity instead of emphasizing the essentials of
faith and love.

■ Problems in the Community ■

The existence of these distinct groups helps us to appreciate some of the problems faced by the Johannine community. In John 9:22 the reference to expulsion from the synagogue comes not from the ministry of Jesus but from the period of the Johannine community. Eventually Christians had to make a decisive break with the synagogue. This decisive step on the part of Judaism forced the crypto-Christians to make a decision for or against the new way of Jesus.

The presence of followers of John the Baptist, who claimed that John, not Jesus, was the messiah, prompted the Johannine community to downplay the importance of John and depict him not as the Baptizer (the term is not used) but as a Christian witness who bore testimony to Jesus. They faced this problem by denying it. Jesus alone is the messiah.

Docetism, an early Christian heresy, held that the body of Jesus was not really a human body. The Johannine gospel attempted to counteract this belief by emphasizing the reality of the body of Jesus in his ministry. Jesus thirsts; he is hungry; he becomes tired. Even after the resurrection he eats with his disciples. The Son of God took flesh and lived and died humanly.

Gnosticism, that strange system of beliefs that created an intellectual elite by promising salvation through the communication of secret knowledge, also caused problems for this community. Gnostic influences can clearly be found in this gospel. "The truth will make you free" (8:32) seems Gnostic. Jesus teaches what he has learned from his Father, for he is the light of the world. This seems at least esoteric if not Gnostic. Moreover, he says, "I am the way the truth and the light" (14:6). Since the community lived in such a diverse environment, some of these influences would find their way into the gospel. But the author never departs from the basic thrust of salvation, through the communication of the Spirit, which comes only through love and the death on the cross. "When I am lifted up, I will draw all people to myself" (12:32). Gnosticism may offer some contribution to Christianity but at heart Gnosticism is false. Love, not knowledge, conquers all.

The community also faced problems with other Christian communities. By the end of the first century the Christian church had developed sufficiently to institutionalize certain ecclesial offices. The more charismatic type of church order gave way to an established authority and hierarchy. Certain church leaders traced their office in the church to Peter and laid claim to a share in the authority of Jesus himself. The Johannine community, sectarian to begin with, came into conflict with these interpretations of Christianity and attempted to offer its own formula for church order. The Third Letter of John, verses 9–10, implies that other Christian communities had difficulties with the Johannine community.

> I wrote to the church but Diotrophes who loves to dominate does not acknowledge us. Therefore if I come, I will draw attention to what he is doing, spreading evil nonsense about us. And not content with that, he will not receive the brothers, hindering those who wish to do so and expelling them from the church.

The interpretation of Christian faith by the community of the Beloved Disciple differed from other early communities, and thus disagreements and dissensions inevitably created a troubled existence for its members. They had their own understanding of Jesus and interpreted that tradition to suit their own needs.

■   Johannine Dualism   ■

The Fourth Gospel employs dualistic language: light and darkness, truth and falsehood, above and below, good and evil, life and death, God and the world. Do these concepts come from a Gnostic background or are they rooted in Judaism? Some scholars have presented arguments in favor of the Gnostic origin for this dualism, while others have argued for the essential Jewish origin, especially through the study of the Jewish community of Essenes at Qumran. The same concepts existed in Gnosticism as well as in Qumran, and since the Johannine community flourished in a mixed social order, no one satisfactory answer can be found to this question of origin. The Gnostic concept of life may very well have influenced the gospel. The general agreement in terminology in both the Qumran scrolls and the Fourth Gospel also shows a familiarity by the Johannine community of the thought present in the writings of the Qumran community even if no direct literary dependence seems evident.

■   Gnosticism and Qumran   ■

The relationship between Gnosticism and the thought of Qumran has not been studied sufficiently. The discussion on the possible origin of Johannine dualism in one or the other milieu overlooks the Gnostic elements that were also part of the Qumran experience. The life of the Essenes at Qumran could be seen as an early form of Jewish Gnosticism, which would have contributed significantly to the emergence of the later Christian Gnosticism. The eclectic and sectarian form of heterodox Judaism of Qumran best represents the intellectual environment from which the author of the Fourth Gospel discovered some of the language and concepts used to articulate the unusual formulation of the Christian message.

When contemporary students of John read of the struggle between light and darkness, good and evil, the world below and the world above, they recognize these as ideas coming from a group of people removed from the mainstream of social life. They expected to experience salvation through a personal relationship with Jesus, God's envoy. The Qumran community withdrew from the orthodox way of Jewish life to a desert community in which they were dependent upon a teacher and awaited expectantly for the coming of the messiah or messiahs who would usher in the final relationship to God. The Johannine community also lived slightly apart from the mainstream of developing Christianity and accepted a Christian faith that allowed for little compromise. Its members too awaited a fulfillment, but a fulfillment that had substantially begun through the coming of Jesus, the incarnation of the Word of God.

John and the Synoptics

Any appreciation of the milieu of the Fourth Gospel must also include some investigation of the relationship between this gospel and the other three. Mark, Matthew and Luke existed at this period of history and were accepted as authentic expressions of the Jesus tradition. Did the Johannine community use these gospels in any way?

Often in the past people looked upon the Fourth Gospel as an effort by the author to fill in what was missing in the synoptics. Today, such a theory lies buried in the history of interpretation. A careful study of the gospel, for most scholars, shows no literary dependence on the other three. The Fourth Gospel seems closer to Luke and Mark than Matthew, but even the common elements among John and Luke and Mark show no evidence of a direct literary dependence. In spite of the efforts of some to show a close literary dependency upon Mark by the author of the Fourth gospel, not much enthusiasm exists for such a position. The author of John most likely did not know the other three gospels. The similarities can be explained by a similar oral tradition that lies behind all of the gospels.

The plan of the last gospel, however, does conform generally to that of Mark: Galilee, Jerusalem, death and resurrection, the sending of the Spirit. But how the author presents this basic plan differs significantly. For example, the synoptic gospels have Jesus going to Jerusalem only once, just before his death. John has Jesus traveling to Jerusalem many times.

The Order of Events

The order of events changes in this gospel. The cleansing of the temple, for example, takes place at the beginning of the ministry of Jesus rather than at the end, just before his death. The evangelist can situate this event here for, unlike the synoptics, John has Jesus visiting Jerusalem several times. Thus, he can locate the cleansing at one of several visits.

The gospel also places the crucifixion on a different day. The Fourth Gospel sets the crucifixion on the day of preparation for the Passover, at the time the lambs would have been slain in the temple in preparation for the Passover meal. For the synoptics, Jesus celebrated the Passover meal with his disciples and then died the following day. Which gospel is historically accurate remains unknown. The Fourth Gospel may well have Jesus dying at the very time of the slaughter of the lambs for Passover for theological and symbolic reasons, but perhaps that is when it actually happened.

The Words of Jesus

The author also presents the words of Jesus in a manner different from the synoptics. All of the evangelists adapted the actual words of Jesus to suit the needs of the individual communities. The authors of the synoptic gospels, however, had a more conservative approach in preserving the historical words of Jesus. In the Fourth Gospel half of the verses are discourses unknown to the synoptics. This author also seems to arrange and alter the words of Jesus with greater freedom. He presents the teaching of Jesus, but the words are those of the evangelist or, perhaps, of the Beloved Disciple who liked to preach homilies about Jesus.

The Beloved Disciple or the evangelist, however, did not just create these discourses of Jesus. The so-called Johannine thunderbolt in the synoptics sounds like the gospel of John:

> All things have been delivered to me by my Father and no one knows the Son except the Father, and no one knows the Father except the Son and anyone to whom the Son chooses to reveal him (Mt 11:27).

This supports the opinion that the basic ideas in the gospel of John are also present in the synoptic tradition, though in a germinal or indirect fashion. The Fourth Gospel represents a creative remembering of the Jesus tradition that adapts the teaching of Jesus to the needs of a particular church community.

The Risen Lord Speaks

Throughout this gospel, in distinction to that of the other evangelists, the author often presents Jesus as speaking from eternity. The risen Lord addresses his followers more than does the historical Jesus. The teaching is rooted in the earthly Jesus but carries greater development. When the author, for example, narrates the multiplication of the loaves in chapter 6, he presents the event in the context of Jesus as Incarnate Wisdom as well as Jesus present in the eucharist. This differs significantly from Mark's presentation of the same miracle in chapters 6 and 8, in which Mark presents Jesus as the shepherd who feeds his flock and offers the food of the eschatological banquet.

Miracles/Signs

All of the miracles of Jesus take on a different nuance in this gospel. In the synoptics they cause wonder. In the Fourth Gospel they become signs, deeds of the earthly Jesus. They involve faith in him not as just another miracle worker but carry as well a pledge of the future outpouring of the Spirit. The signs point to who Jesus is and what he expects from those who see or participate in the miracles.

■ Christology ■

The Jesus in this gospel differs significantly from the Jesus of the synoptics. He is never without his glory, and this his followers have seen: "And we have seen his glory, glory as of the only Son from the Father" (1:14). In the earlier gospels the authors offered no hint of pre-existence. In Philippians Paul refers to pre-existence in a veiled manner (Phil 2:6), but for John the Word was with God from the beginning. Even when the Word became flesh, the Word remained in the bosom of the Father (1:18).

Since Jesus speaks from eternity, he knows everything. He knew Nathanael under the fig tree (1:48); he knew the Samaritan woman's marital status (4:17–18); he knew his betrayer (6:70–71); he knew when his hour had come to depart from this world (13:1); he was aware of all that would befall him as he was apprehended in the garden (18:4); and finally, knowing that he had accomplished all, he uttered, "I thirst" to fulfill the scriptures and handed over his Spirit (19:28). No wonder he caused misunderstanding for Nicodemus, the Samaritan woman and his disciples. The author did not set out to correct or amplify the synoptics, but while he accepted a common oral tradition, he developed his own approach to the Jesus tradition, one which was suited to the needs of his particular Christian community.

Conclusion

This survey of the milieu of the Fourth Gospel, after studying various sections of the gospel, should make it evident that the gospel is syncretistic; its community was sectarian; it flourished within a Christian environment that experienced internal as well as external problems; it had its opponents and critics; it borrowed ideas and terminology from the heterodox Judaism of the Qumran community as well as Old Testament theology; it relied on an oral tradition that was similar to the synoptics, especially Luke and Mark, but in the end it produced a document far different from any other gospel. The community's experience included current religious motifs but also had, of necessity, to deal with philosophical, political, sociological and psychological elements. Freedom, individuality, clustering around a charismatic teacher called the Beloved Disciple, the experience of separateness, all are involved with psychology as well as sociology—and each element finds some expression in this gospel.

The work of recent scholarship has focused these influences, and thus students can better understand the gospel if they keep the milieu in mind. Reading the gospel reveals the currents described herein and helps us to appreciate the genius and the value of this authentic witness to the meaning of Jesus.

Suggestions for Reflection

1. How does the knowledge of the Johannine community help in understanding the gospel?
2. Why is this called a gospel when it is so unlike the other gospels?
3. Do the various problems that the Johannine community faced in its life continue to cause concern today?
4. What problems in this community are similar to the problems of Christianity today?
5. Does Gnosticism have any value today?
6. How does this analysis of the origin of the gospel affect the understanding of inspiration?
7. Do you like the Johannine community? Why or why not?

12.

The Beloved Disciple

Five times the Beloved Disciple is explicitly mentioned in the gospel of John. On two other occasions in the final chapter (21:23, 24) "this disciple" is used, clearly referring to the Beloved Disciple. Some attempt to identify him as well with the unknown disciple in chapter 1:35. Most also identify him with the unknown disciple in 18:15. He speaks only twice: "Who is it, Lord?" (13:25) and "It is the Lord" (21:7).

Nowhere in the gospel is the name John ever mentioned, and yet from the second to the twentieth century most Christians have concluded that the author is one of the twelve: John, the son of Zebedee. As recent as thirty years ago within the Roman Catholic tradition Raymond Brown in his commentary and Rudolph Schnackenburg in the first volume of his commentary (but not the third) identified the author in this traditional manner. In his third volume Schnackenburg in an appendix writes of the Beloved Disciple as not one of the twelve and probably a follower of Jesus from Jerusalem. Brown, in his now well-established *The Community of the Beloved Disciple,* joins Schnackenburg in separating the author from the twelve apostles. Neither Brown nor Schnackenburg—nor most other contemporary commentators—seeks to identify this unknown author. He is just one of the unnamed disciples in chapter 21:2.

■ Identity ■

Some, however, still seek to identify this unknown author. In 1992 Joseph Grassi in *The Secret Identity of the Beloved Disciple* studied five candidates as the possible author of the gospel: John, the son of Zebedee; Lazarus; John Mark; John the Presbyter; and the possibility of a literary type rather than a historical figure. In that same year the German exegete W. Schmithals added the following to Grassi's list: the rich young ruler; a beloved brother of Jesus; the unknown disciple of Mark 14:51–52; Andrew; and Nathanael. Two years later A. Culpepper examined eleven possibilities, adding to some of the above Matthias, Paul and Benjamin. He also adds that perhaps the Beloved Disciple symbolizes gentile Christianity (a position that was offered by A. Kragerud in 1959) or an itinerant and prophetic community or the author of the epistles. In fact, over the years more than twenty possibilities have been offered, the most recent by James Charlesworth, who not only offers a thorough study of all of the above possibilities but offers his own opinion that the Beloved Disciple was Thomas, one of the twelve.

Does it make any difference? Does the identity of the Beloved Disciple contribute to the understanding of the gospel and the contemporary church, or is this just another exercise for scholars to use to fill up pages of scholarly periodicals and books? With so many possibilities can anyone ever hope to offer a definitive answer?

Whatever one may accept concerning the actual identity of this unknown disciple, some conclusions from the gospel itself about its author affect the interpretations of the gospel. Although he may always remain anonymous, he is not without character, personality and contours. Something similar may be said of the community from which he came or which he possibly founded.

The Passages

By now the reader is familiar with the passages in which the Beloved Disciple appears. Whether he can also be identified with the unnamed disciple in chapters 1:37 and 18:15 remains uncertain. Most identify him with the latter but not with the former.

13:23–26: He is at the Last Supper close to Jesus.
19:25–27: He stands at the foot of the cross with the mother of Jesus.
20:2–10: He outruns Peter to the tomb and believes.
21:7: He recognizes Jesus.
21:20: Peter questions Jesus concerning him.
21:23–24: The Beloved Disciple has died.

■ The Origin of the Passages ■

The response to the possible origin of these passages of course depends on one's opinion with regard to authorship. If the Beloved Disciple is the author of the gospel, it seems unlikely he would have spoken of himself as the Beloved Disciple. Most admit the gospel went through various editions with different writers or editors. So are these passages from the first edition written by the Beloved Disciple or a first edition written by another hand, or were they added when chapter 21 was added or at some time in between? Were they coming from the life of Jesus or from the needs of the community? Are they part literary to symbolize a historical person or completely literary, added to suit the needs of the final editor and/or the needs of the community?

■ The Inspirer of the Gospel ■

Most likely the passages come from an author or editor who was not the Beloved Disciple. They are additions to what might have been an early edition of the gospel written primarily for the needs of the community. Although many have problems accepting that the Beloved Disciple would call himself that, no problem exists with his followers calling him by that title even in his lifetime.

■ Methodology ■

Today, New Testament exegesis involves as many types of methodology as one can find students of the New Testament. The days of complete historicity are gone, as are the days of a purist historical-critical approach. Literary methodologies, the use of sociology and psychology as well as reader response methodologies have all added to the ever-expanding meaning of the New Testament. Throughout this work the historical-critical method as well as the phenomenological method with some touches of anthropology and literary methods have been utilized.

■ Historicity ■

Anyone studying ancient documents must pay attention to the flux of history. Everyone is now caught in the current of the late twentieth century. Objectivity eludes those living in this period as much as it eluded those trying to retell the story of the Exodus and Moses in the tenth century before Christ and those who attempted to pass on the Jesus tradition at the end of the first century. Life itself and surely thought, speech and even the written word are always more heteromorphous than homeomorphous. Radical temporality characterizes everything.

How much of the Jesus in the Fourth Gospel actually goes back to the historical Jesus? No one may ever know. The reality comes from the meaning and effect, not just the historicity. The radical temporality involves Jesus, how he was understood, how the evangelist wanted to present Jesus, how this presentation was understood by the Johannine community and then how people today understand the story.

Historicity and the Fourth Gospel

How much of this can be applied to the gospels and in particular to the gospel of John? More should be understood as historicity than many might want, but with less complete objectivity precisely because historicity is a river; there is less historicity than others might want for the same reason. When considered both phenomenologically and anthropologically, the story means more than the facts. If the Beloved Disciple is so close to Jesus in this gospel, and if he is presented as superior to Peter, even if this has little historical reality for the time of Jesus, it must have had great historical value for the community of the gospel. But if the gospel shows such interest in details and if the community demanded acceptance, then somehow the testimony comes from an eyewitness. Some history and some literary creation make the most sense in analyzing this gospel both about Jesus and his ministry as well as about this community and the Beloved Disciple.

History, society, language and culture all contribute to what should be preserved and how it should be retold. Since humanity differs from age to age and from culture to culture, then an individual's understanding of reality or a community's understanding, even of such a thing as a sacred revelation or a sacred book, varies relative to historical situations. What the community of the Fourth Gospel grasped and presented in a text becomes relativized to the particular community. Its members remembered what they wanted and told the story as they saw fit from their own perspective. Of course, the same is true for any of the gospels or any book in the

Bible. The phenomenon remains today, and being aware of that can help to give insights into the actual community.

■ Phenomenology and Anthropology ■

The phenomenologist remains open to all that is not the subject and tries to integrate and understand based on a double subjectivity: personal and the subjectivity of whatever is not the subject. What is offered is accepted and then studied on the basis of personal experience and by allowing the text to interpret itself. The anthropologist tries to see some relationship with how people live and lived and act and acted, then and now, forever acknowledging the river of historicity and radical temporality. The literary analyst and sociologist tries to draw conclusions based on form and structure and relationships of groups and individuals, also accepting the limitations of historical flux.

Contours of the Beloved Disciple and the Author

With these methodologies in use, since the author shows little interest in Galilee he probably was not a Galilean. Fishermen are usually practical people. This gospel seems more contemplative. He was probably not a fisherman. The author has a good command of Greek and knows Aramaic and fills his work with irony and subtlety and even a forensic element. The author was "smart." He also seems to have little interest in the apocalyptic. His eschatology is more realized than future. Jesus does not suffer in this gospel. He probably did not like suffering. Yet he acknowledged that Jesus died by crucifixion, so he had some thoughts on suffering and those thoughts are presented in a positive manner. The Samaritans in this gospel appear in a good light and are treated with respect. Jews, in general, are not. He seems to be superior to Peter and to the rest of the twelve, since the word *twelve* is mentioned only four times and never in a very positive light (Jn 6:67, 70, 71; 20:24). He seems to know the geography of Samaria and Judea. He probably was known to the high priest's court in Jerusalem. He likes to give homilies and pass them off as the words of Jesus. Thus far this analysis has moved back and forth between the Beloved Disciple and the author. Such is inevitable, since no one can be quite sure just what came from whom.

Of course someone could also say that he, whether Beloved Disciple or author or both, was a Galilean fisherman but did not like being one so he went to a good school and learned Greek and so forth. While admitting the eternal flux of life, thought, speech and writing, some foundationalism must remain. Whatever the ultimate limitations on understanding the Beloved Disciple and this community, some sense of universal nature perdures, even while it is ceaselessly affected by a historical and hermeneutical consciousness.

To return to the Beloved Disciple and his gospel, he is not just one disciple among many, but rather he seems identified with the tradition of this gospel even if he probably did not write it. The author presents him as a believer. No doubt! He follows Jesus even to the cross; he is referred to as beloved; and he bears testimony. Each has some relevance to the historicity of both the Jesus tradition and the community.

Believer, Follower, Beloved, Witness

As believer he sees the empty tomb and believes (20:6–9), in contrast to Peter. He is also superior to Thomas, who needs to see physically (20:25). *No* doubt ever seems to cloud his relationship to Jesus.

As a follower (disciple), he remained with Jesus to the end, joined only by the mother of Jesus and some additional women followers. Prior to the cross he followed Jesus to the court of the high priest (18:15), and since he appears in chapter 21 he followed Jesus after the resurrection as well. Once he became a follower of Jesus he remained faithful to him always.

He is also beloved. This implies an intimacy with Jesus that is completed with the responsibility of taking care of the mother of Jesus (19:26–27). The author singles him out for special affection for Jesus and from Jesus. Of all of the disciples he holds a special place in the affections of Jesus.

Finally, he bears testimony, witness. The bond of love qualifies the Beloved Disciple to be a witness of Jesus to others so that they might believe and love. He has witnessed (19:35), and his testimony remains as the gospel. Since the gospel remains as part of the New Testament and will always be so, the testimony of the Beloved Disciple continues for every age.

The Community of the Gospel

The community of the Beloved Disciple has been called a maverick community. It taught faith in Jesus and the love of the brethren as the only essential elements of Christianity. It has been accused of being anti-authority, anti-sacrament, anti-church. In fact, the community was individualistic but not exclusively. It believed in sacraments but only as expressions of faith. It accepted authority, other than that of the Beloved Disciple and the Paraclete, only if those in authority loved Jesus and were willing to die for the community. It emphasized the here and now, human relationships and a realized eschatology. All of this is readily recognized in reading the gospel. This community clearly maintained a different approach to the Jesus tradition than other communities of the New Testament. It had its own grasp of the meaning of Jesus. It reached into the river of historicity and took out what it wanted.

The Word of God and the Words of Jesus

Each of the authors of the gospels makes free with the words of Jesus. Even Mark, the earliest, is willing to add actual words of Jesus to interpret the parable of the sower. Matthew feels no compunction in adding the direct command to Peter in chapter 16 and the solemn sending out in 28. Luke also freely adds his own words to the words of Jesus. Even if the author of John takes greater freedom with the words of Jesus than the others, they all add their own words and the words of their communities to the words of Jesus. They all experience the essential limitations of life, thought and speech and add their own truth mediated by historical flux, community needs and norms and cultural warrants.

If Jesus was the Word of God Incarnate, and if Jesus as Word remained with the community, then surely the early community spoke the Word of God for their own needs, assured that they were speaking the one Word of God made man in the life of Jesus. Both phenomenologically and anthropologically verbal inspiration means that individuals could and did add to the words of Jesus as they saw necessary precisely because of ever-mutable humanity. The community accepted and then integrated the Word of God into its own times and places and needs. Understanding the Jesus tradition in this gospel offers a window of insight into the life of the community.

■ The Community of the Beloved Disciple ■ and the Beloved Disciple

The study of this gospel can help us to imagine this Christian community at the end of the first century. It comprised a mixed group hardly able to get along without some overarching person of great charism. There were half Christians and half Jews; low christologists and high christologists; Gnostics and half Gnostics; superintelligent and barely educable; some emphasizing only divinity and others only humanity. Just think of a greatly mixed community that also had problems with other Christian communities regarding such matters as authority, essentials, sacraments and an individual who tried to keep them together. The phenomenon has existed in every era in every religious tradition. Like other communities since then, the community of the Beloved Disciple had its own understanding of Jesus and his gospel.

1. Its members wanted to be accepted by other Christian communities just as they were. They claimed they had such a right, for their leader was present with Jesus and could pick and choose from the river of historicity in the Jesus tradition.

2. They tried to preserve what was essential to the Jesus tradition, never forgetting the role of faith and love of the brethren. The river continues to flow, but there is a river.

3. They wished to make a contribution to early and then future Christianity. Their witness had value and belonged. The document from the community should be part of the early Christian heritage.

4. They refused to be marginalized even as they *were* marginalized. They did not mind being at the doorway of the then developing church, but they refused to be outside.

5. They were willing to compromise, but not in what they believed were essentials.

6. They accepted the complexity of a individual human life and thus the greater complexity of communal life. Multiplicity and variety characterized their community, and no efforts to oversimplify ever helped. Jesus himself was too complex. Life, humanity, never remains static. Rocking and shuttering in the midst of history is the only way the individual and the community can cope with the ever-changing radical temporality.

7. They recognized the role of a charismatic type of authority and leadership and acknowledged its limitations. The charismatic

leader often anticipates the rocking and shuttering but at times can cause the same.

8. They created a gospel expressing all of the above, and they disappeared from history because they lacked the means of continuity. The river went on and swallowed them. They had trouble dealing with ordinary human sin.

This most unusual community, with its most unusual leader, the Beloved Disciple, disappeared from history. Only the gospel remains. Just paying attention to the words of the gospel offers much in knowing about both leader and community. How they lived and how they acted preached the gospel of Jesus. They made it their own.

So who was the Beloved Disciple? No one really knows. He probably was a combination of historical figure and ideal follower. The story is more important than the fact. His community lacked clear lines of authority other than the Beloved Disciple and the Spirit. The leadership was spontaneous, not just tolerating but accepting all people. Both he and his community lived on the edge of early Christianity, wanting to be part of the group and yet wanting to preserve some sense of unique identity in this early period. Today, he remains unknown. It is better. Let the community also live in the shadows of history. The testimony of the gospel is enough. The Beloved Disciple continues to bear testimony whoever he was. Read the story.

Suggestions for Reflection

1. Does radical temporality make any sense? How can you avoid relativizing the relative?
2. Authority in the church often has its problems. What value does the testimony of the Beloved Disciple offer for understanding authority in the church today?
3. Is there a conflict between a more charismatic approach to Christianity and a more hierarchical approach? How can both function?
4. Does it make any difference if the author remains anonymous?
5. Why might the developing church have had problems with the community of the Beloved Disciple?
6. With so many people using so many differing methodologies in interpreting the New Testament, does this just cause more confusion?

7. How does this analysis of a gospel affect your understanding of inspiration?

8. How does the theology of this gospel affect the community, and vice versa?

13.

The Gospel According to John Today

■ Individualism ■

Society vacillates between individualism and collectivism. In most periods of history the extremes are not so evident as the pendulum continues its swing. Recently, however, the emphasis on individualism has waxed strong, especially in the United States. People live their own lives, make their own decisions, often not based on any consideration of the needs of others or of the communities in which they are members. Individualism permeates every aspect of life: education, politics, the economy, the family and religion.

The recent interest in Eastern religions is individualistic, as is New Age spirituality. The new spiritualities outshine any organized religion. The individual develops a close relationship to God on a deeply personal level. The lives of those who follow these Eastern traditions or the New Age movement change considerably. God becomes integrated into a life that finds meaning in the integration. The spiritual richness gives rise to enrichment of the total person.

The Charismatic Movement

The Charismatic Movement within Christianity has also encouraged an individual faith commitment to Jesus as personal savior. The individual becomes aware of his or her need to relate to Jesus on a deeply personal level and grows in the awareness of salvation as personally experienced. Often those in the Charismatic Movement have been baptized in the Spirit of Jesus and know that the Lord has a personal interest in their lives. Jesus knows them by name, calls them to himself and promises the joys that only a personal commitment can create. The believer then leads others to

150

Jesus so that they too may experience this joy. A community develops in the process based on the personal relationship to Jesus.

Reaction to Collectivism

These movements that stress individualism and appeal to individuals both as members of society and as members of the church surely are in no small part a reaction to the emphasis on the collective that characterized both society and the church for a long period of time. The response should have been expected. Recall the education that characterized the schooling of most adults: the controlled program for all, based solely on chronological age. Gradually people learned that such a system was detrimental to intellectual growth and change set in. Now education caters to individual needs and levels.

Religion encourages people to make a personal commitment to some ideal and live accordingly. The Charismatic Movement encourages Christians to make a personal commitment to Jesus as a personal savior. Individuals become aware of their need to relate to Jesus on a deeply personal level and grow in the awareness of salvation as actually experienced. When they experience baptism in the Spirit they know that the Lord has entered their life. The Good Shepherd knows each by name; they hear his voice and follow him, knowing the great joy of being with the Lord. New Age spiritualities and Eastern religions also encourage the individual to make a profession in an ideal and live accordingly.

Roman Catholicism

All of these movements with their emphasis on the individual stand in stark contrast with the recent past especially of Roman Catholicism. The Catholic Church stressed the community. Theology developed on the concept of a common good. Directives, rules and regulations were universal in scope and application. Uniformity in doctrine imposed uniformity in thought and practice. The community was fundamental. On that basis decisions could be made for all individuals. If a person wished to participate in the life of the community, his or her only choice was to accept what was imposed from above. The alternative meant leaving the community. The Roman Church may never have been in theory a monolith, but in practice it was just that. The Caiphas principle prevailed: the individual will be sacrificed for the sake of the community.

The results were unfortunate. Intellectual activity died; adults were treated like children; regulations did not take into consideration changes in society or different cultures; opportunities for enrichment to the church were lost. Often people became aware of their personal needs and found it impossible to remain within the church community. The shock in religious life of both men and women resulting from the changes in the Second Vatican Council and the acceptance of individual talents and needs continues to reverberate in church and society today.

To blame the church or church leaders for many unfortunate results coming from an extreme collectivism helps no one. The church has always suffered or gained from societal influences. If society functioned with an overdose of collectivity, the church felt the effects of such force in its own structure and practice. The structure of the church, with the concentration of power in the hierarchy, heightened the tendency to control individuals and treat them as only parts of the whole. But structure is needed.

Individualism in Roman Catholicism

The causes and sources for the unrest in the Roman Catholic community following the Second Vatican Council may be more numerous and intangible than historians can enumerate. Part of the unrest may be due to the past emphasis on the collective and the reaction with a strong sense of individualism especially as this has characterized Western society. The collapse of communism also has ushered in a strong individualism in Eastern Europe. The church often failed to deal effectively with the hopes, expectations and needs of the individual believer in both East and West. The results of this failure grow each day in both societies.

Many people feel drowned in the sea of bureaucracy. Finally some decided to make their presence and needs known. Thus began the period of individualism in the church, and it continues, whether dealing with women's issues or shared decision-making or matters of individual sexual morality.

Within Roman Catholicism this age of individualism has certainly made its mark. Church officials often seem to spend more time defending the rights and the authority of the church in light of the demands of individual members of the church. Many Roman Catholics consider their consciences as the judges of morality even when their personal conclusions differ substantially from what has been the official and historical position of the church. The individual considers his or her conscience the final arbiter and acts accordingly. People also refuse to be driven from the church and proclaim their general allegiance, if not faithfulness to all the particulars.

Problems and Individualism

But, as might be expected, all the problems of society and the church have not been resolved with the advent of individualism. One set of problems has only shifted to another. Both extremes are detrimental to the position of Christianity and its mission as well as to society. The tension remains in the church as well as in society. With regard to the church, should the individual be primary or not? Must the community override the needs of the person in some circumstances? How can the church be true to its structure and still allow for the needs of the individual in the church? Is it possible for the church to maintain a creative tension between the individual and the community, each interacting and finding a resolution that will encourage the individual and at the same time not harm the needs of the church community and structure?

Individualism, Collectivism and the Fourth Gospel

The study of the gospel of John will not solve all of the problems facing the church, but this gospel can offer some guidance. If the gospel shows indications of similar problems in the early church, and if the gospel remains the Word of God, then the contemporary church may find in this document some insights into contemporary problems. Final solutions, however, will always remain elusive, for even the church has to learn to live with a perennial tension with radical temporality.

■ Individual and Community in John ■

Throughout the gospel the Johannine community struggled with individualism and reacted against a strong collectivism. The teaching in this gospel stressed individual commitment to the Lord as fundamental. The author saw a need for the collectivity characterized not by authority and structure but by a mutual love of the brethren. The gospel places communal elements in their rightful perspective. Ritual, the celebration of baptism and the eucharist, mean nothing unless they express the hearts of people committed to Jesus. Authority is necessary and possible, but not the type that lords it over others. A common faith and a profound love of the brethren binds the community together with bonds more powerful than established authority and hierarchical structure. The gospel contains a tension resolved in favor of neither the individual nor the community.

Christianity can never really function properly if it is based only on organization, order and control, a system of doctrine and a code of ethics. When a community settles for a formalized ritual and fails to encourage and accept personal involvement and commitment, the church teeters on its demise. When church authority fails to consider the needs, expectations, and hopes of the individual believers, its authority is suspect. The Johannine community knew the pitfalls other Christian communities experienced and tried to give its own testimony to the essentials of the Jesus tradition. Without the individual believers, the church loses its foundation. The gospel even admits of differences in faith. Some doubted, some lacked full understanding, some were impetuous and some even fell from faith. Jesus accepted them, and the Beloved Disciple and his community made room for them.

The Organized Church

The Johannine tradition did not oppose an organized and hierarchical church. Evidently in its time some traced their authority to Peter. The final editor recognized the legitimacy of such claims but also pointed out the conditions under which the authority should be exercised. From the perspective of the twentieth century, Christianity could not have survived without order and organization. The author of the final chapter recognized this as well and knew that at times the individual must cede his or her rights to the needs of the community. But not always.

Today, decrees, regulations and organization mean little unless they come from people with the faith commitment to the Lord, people with a willingness to die for one of the brethren. This must be especially visible in the leaders of the church, those who share in the authority of the Good Shepherd. Following the example of Jesus, church leaders lead other followers in the commitment in faith and in the love of the brethren.

■ Faith, Love and Good Order ■

The contemporary world pays attention when the heart of Christianity is proclaimed and professed in church structures. The bond of love and the faith commitment build up the community. At times some will become so overwhelmed by the power of faith and love that they will overlook good order. They forget what the daily operation of a community of almost a billion people entails. Yet they too must be allowed their rightful place in the church so that the testimony of the community of the Beloved Disciple will continue. Such individuals stand as beacons to all members of the church, reminding them—and chiding them, if necessary—that faith and love create the Christian church.

■ Personal Faith Commitment ■

The gospel stresses a personal relationship to Jesus. Before all else the individual must make a faith commitment to the Lord. The study of Johannine christology shows how essential that response is, for it creates the community of Jesus, the church. The position of individuals in this gospel adds additional weight to the argument that the author was struggling with the need to emphasize the role and place of the individual believer for the good of the church.

■ Sacraments ■

The Johannine community also wished to place the sacraments, which belong to both the group and the individual, in their proper perspective. Ritual means nothing unless it expresses the faith of committed people. Baptism and the celebration of the eucharist express a reality already present: faith and love. With these as the foundation, the ritual expression takes on a power and a beauty that transforms.

■ Love in the Community ■

The Christian community will remain together based upon this common faith and impelled by this faith into a profound love of the brethren. The need for love of the brethren further emphasizes that faith without the fruit of love destroys the initial faith. Bearing fruit still means to love one another.

The community was aware of the necessity of a communal life, as evidenced in the stories about the Good Shepherd and the flock and the Vine and the Branches. The command of Jesus to love the brethren also witnessed to the need for a mutual relationship among the members. The tension experienced in the lifestyle of the community as it encountered other expressions of Christianity encouraged the Johannine church to maintain the fundamental principles upon which it had based its following of Jesus. This same tension also allowed its members to admit the presence of a hierarchical and authoritarian church. The Gospel According to John preserves the rights of the individual without denying the purpose or reality of the community. The gospel stresses the fundamentals of the life of the community and places some of the communal elements in their proper perspective.

For individual members of the church the gospel offers support for a renewal in faith with the injunction that this alone is primary but without undermining the present needs of the community. The individual does not hold an exclusive mandate, nor may the community exercise absolute control. The tension between both remains.

■ The One Word of God ■

Historically the enthusiasts in the history of the church called this gospel their own just as the Gnostics in the second century used this document as their private possession. Historically those responsible for the hierarchical church have tended to call the gospel of Matthew, Luke/Acts and the pastoral epistles their special mandate. Any choice of one book in the New Testament as an exclusive guide invites disaster. The Word of God addressed to people in human words comprise one Bible. The church rests upon a living out of the Bible, not one book of that Bible. If the present church turns to the witness of the Johannine community and recognizes in this writing an expression of age-old questions and some possible responses, the church will recognize how a particular book can be of greater help at one moment in history than another.

The Community of the Beloved Disciple

The community of the Beloved Disciple at the end of the first century comprised a mixed group. It had problems with other Christian communities regarding such matters as authority, essentials, sacraments and an individual who tried to keep them together. It wanted acceptance; it wished to preserve what was essential and to maintain its own traditions, making its own contribution to Christianity. It could accept compromise, especially since life was so complicated. It liked the charismatic element in the church, even if this marginalized its members and caused them trouble.

This most unusual community with its most unusual leader, the Beloved Disciple, disappeared from history. Only the gospel remains. But this unusual document still gives testimony today. The gospel offers guidance for contemporary church communities.

Various Christian communities need to be accepted by other Christian communities just as they are. This is most evident with Eastern and Western Christianity. Each reaches into the river of history and takes out what is of value.

Essentials are more important than accidentals. Faith and love still constitute the true meaning of Jesus and his tradition. The incidentals and accidentals of centuries never should obscure faith and love. History makes evident what is more temporal and what has some semblance of continuity.

Both individuals and individual Christian communities in different cultures, different periods of history and so on make a contribution. The maverick community of the Beloved Disciple managed to have its gospel included in the canon of the New Testament. This very different testimony to Jesus continues.

Marginalizing any segment of the community impoverishes all. Yet the marginalizing itself can emphasize a forgotten truth: a blessing and curse. Marginalizing belongs in the flux of history. Both the marginalized and those who are not marginalized have something to offer to each other and to receive from each other.

Compromise helps. Radical temporality demands it but not always. Wisdom does not reside only in the homes of the mighty. History and faith give direction in deciding when to compromise.

Life is too complex, and all still live in history. Too much gray perdures; there is too little black and white, in spite of all of the efforts to proclaim one thing or another as definitive. Mutual efforts to understand and communicate not only make the complexity apparent but often can lead toward solutions.

Charismatic leadership is good but not perfect. It does not last. It can be most creative as well as most destructive. The church needs it, but it also needs the structure of authority and organization.

Over the centuries many other unknowns, like the Beloved Disciple and his community, both women and men, have lived the story and made their contribution. Being marginalized has always been both a gift and curse for those who follow Jesus. Living the essentials and ignoring the nonessentials have not always been well received by all members of the church, but such people have made their contribution. The wonder of Christianity and the New Testament includes four very different gospels and works attributed to Paul as different as Galatians and Romans and the pastorals. Somewhere in the Bible, in the midst of confusion and division and differences, with faith and love as primary, the lesson lies. The Beloved Disciple and his community continue to bear testimony— whoever he was, whoever they were, and wherever they lived. The testimony will remain until the Lord returns. It was written that you may believe and may continue to believe that "Jesus is the Messiah, the Son of God, so that through this faith you may have life in his name" (Jn 20:31).

Suggestions for Reflection

1. The conflict between individualism and the group often characterizes society as well as the church. Does the conflict still exist in society and in the church? Is this helpful or not?

2. If Roman Catholics make their own decisions based on conscience, how does this affect authority in the church? Does the gospel of John offer any guidance?

3. What is the value of rules and regulations in the church? How would the Johannine community react to such control? Is there any way the church can avoid such rules?

4. Would the Johannine community have felt at home at the Second Vatican Council or not? What aspects of the conciliar reform would the Johannine community have favored? What aspects would it have opposed?

5. When should the needs of the Christian community override the needs of the individual, and vice versa?

6. If the early church had such struggles, can we expect the struggles ever to end? What can be done in the meantime when faced with these problems?

7. Will stressing the need for a personal relationship to the Lord assist in the problems of the contemporary church? How might this help?

8. Will the love of the brethren radicalize the community? Is this realistic or not? How can a typical parish live such an ideal?

9. How can the concept of church authority be altered? Or does it need to be altered? Does this gospel give any guidance for solving problems of authority?

Appendix:

A Thematic Guide to the Gospel of John

*T*he gospel of John offers one particular approach to the Jesus tradition. Like an observer sitting on the shore and taking from the river whatever is of interest, so the author faces the Jesus tradition inherited and part of personal experience and picks out those elements helpful to his community. From these he writes his gospel.

Faith and love form the foundation for Christianity. Without the personal commitment to Jesus as God's Son, the Lord who gives eternal life, who calls people from darkness, nothing else is possible. Following the example of the Good Shepherd, those who believe take care of the other sheep just as Jesus takes care of the sheep. The love of the brethren must characterize the Christian community, for only in that way can its members remain on the vine and bear fruit.

This last-written gospel invites the reader to enter into the experience of early followers of Jesus and an early church community. For only when individuals encounter the risen Lord can faith become personal.

The Gospel According to John has been studied in a general fashion. Now the reader would do well to read the gospel in its entirety several times. Each time notice in each chapter the principal themes or ideas. Below is a suggested list. Use it as a guide, adding your own comments. Some themes seem to occur in every chapter, for example, belief and life. Notice that other themes are not mentioned so frequently.

Some accuse the gospel of being anti-Semitic. Notice how often Moses and Old Testament themes appear and how often the Jews are presented in a positive light. Notice also when the Jews and the Pharisees are presented in a negative light.

Many individuals move in and out of these chapters. Some are historical figures from the time of Jesus, but others from the history

160

of Israel add their presence. In addition, several groups appear on various occasions. Note all of these personages and how they are portrayed by the author. Moses, for example, appears in five chapters and is named more than once in some of these chapters. Abraham also makes an appearance. Jesus forms the central image; around him circle many different individuals, each having some relationship to Jesus, for in this gospel that alone gives them reason to be mentioned.

Reading the gospel brings insight. The more often the gospel is read, the greater the understanding. Each time you read the gospel, somehow verses jump out never before seen. The gospel continues to bear testimony.

Prologue
The Word and God
Life
Light and darkness
The Role of John [the Baptizer]
The world: how portrayed?
Believe and belief
Grace and truth
Glory
Father and Son

Chapter 1
People present: named and unnamed
Testimony of John [the Baptizer]
Pharisees: how portrayed?
Water and Spirit
Call and reaction of the disciples
Immediate faith
Titles used for Jesus
General comportment and attitude of Jesus
Genesis 28:12

Chapter 2
People present: named and unnamed
Title used for Mary
Wine
Hour
Temple theme
Signs
Which feast?

Jews: how portrayed?
Believe and belief

Chapter 3
People present: named and unnamed
Night and darkness
Titles used for Jesus
Pharisees: how portrayed?
Signs
Dialogue
Words of Nicodemus
Role of the Spirit and Wind
Son of Man
Eternal life
Father and only Son
The world: how portrayed?
Light, darkness, evil and sin
Believe and belief
Light
Baptizing and John
The Spirit and the words of God
Testimony/witness

Chapter 4
People present: named and unnamed
Pharisees: how presented?
Jews: how portrayed?
Samaritans: how portrayed?
Samaritan woman: attitude
Titles used for Jesus by the woman
Dialogue and understanding
Eternal life
Living water
Worship: meaning
Spirit and truth
Disciples and their role
Attitude of Jesus throughout
Believe and belief
Signs
Work of God
Which feast?
Mission: to whom and for what?

Chapter 5
People present: named and unnamed
Which feast?
Jews: how presented?
The works of God
Water
Temple theme
Father and Son: relationship
Eternal life
Judgment
Hour
Testimony/witness
John and his role
Glory
Believe and belief

Chapter 6
People present: named and unnamed
Signs
Which feast?
Actions and words of Jesus with regard to the loaves
"It is I"
Son of Man
Father and Son: relationship
Works of God
The Jews: how portrayed?
Son of Man
Believe and belief
Bread
Life and eternal life
Words used: flesh and blood
Twelve
Holy One

Chapter 7
People present: named and unnamed
Which feast?
Disciples
Brothers of Jesus
Jews: how portrayed?
World: how presented?
The Pharisees and leaders: how portrayed?

Temple theme
Glory
Titles used for Jesus
Seek
Hour
Water and thirst and drink
The role of the Spirit

Chapter 8
People present: named and unnamed
Light and darkness
Testimony/witness
Pharisees: how portrayed?
Judge and judgment
Father/Son: relationship
Hour
Above and below
World: how portrayed?
Believe and belief
Son of Man
"I am"
Word
Free
Sin and the devil
Truth
Glory/glorified
Life and death

Chapter 9
People present: named and unnamed
Titles used by the blind man for Jesus
Attitude of the blind man throughout
Attitude of Jesus throughout
Pharisees and Jews: how portrayed?
Day and night
Light and darkness
Water
See
Believe and belief
Sin and sinner
Disciples

Chapter 10
People present: named and unnamed
Door
Call by name
Hear the voice
Saved
Life
Father and Jesus: relationship
One
Jews: how presented?
Which feast?
God
Believe and belief
Works of God
Witness/testimony
Eternal life
John and his testimony

Chapter 11
People present: named and unnamed
Love
Glory/glorified
Death
Titles used for Jesus
Light and darkness
Day and night
Believe and belief
Dialogue with sisters
Jews and Pharisees: how portrayed?
Resurrection
Eternal life
Attitude of Jesus throughout
Which feast?

Chapter 12
People present: named and unnamed
Jews and Pharisees: how portrayed?
Which feast?
Title used for Jesus
Glory/glorified
Hour
Eternal life

Father and Jesus: relationship
Death
Son of Man
Darkness and light
World: how portrayed?
Signs
Believe and belief
Judgment
Save

Chapter 13
People present: named and unnamed
Hour: meaning
Father and Jesus: relationship
World: how portrayed?
Jews: how portrayed?
Love
Devil
Titles used for Jesus
"I am"
Which feast?
Night
Glory/glorified
Title for disciples
Commandment

Chapter 14
People present: named and unnamed
Believe and belief
Father and Jesus: relationship
Life
Truth
Works
Counselor/Spirit: mission
World: how portrayed?
Peace

Chapter 15
People present: named and unnamed
To bear fruit
Father and Jesus: relationship
Glory/glorified
Love

Title used for disciples
World: how portrayed?
Spirit/Counselor: mission
Title for disciples
Works
Testimony/witness

Chapter 16
People present: how presented?
Hour: meaning
Father and Son: relationship
Truth
Glory/glorified
Attitude of disciples throughout
Joy and sorrow
World: how portrayed?
Love
Believe and belief
Peace
Counselor/Spirit: mission

Chapter 17
Attitude of Jesus throughout
Father and Jesus: relationship
Glory/glorified
Eternal life
Name
World: how portrayed?
Believe and belief
Adjectives used for God
One
Evil one
Sanctify and consecrate
Truth
Relationship among Father, Jesus and disciples

Chapter 18
People present: named and unnamed
Attitude of Jesus throughout
"I am"
Jews and Pharisees: how portrayed?
King and kingship
Testimony/Witness

Truth
Which feast?

Chapter 19
People present: named and unnamed
King and kingship
Sin
Which feast?
Attitude of Jesus throughout
Spirit
Testimony/witness
Truth

Chapter 20
People present: named and unnamed
Time of day
Believe and belief
Titles used for Mary and Jesus
Dialogue content
Relationship among Father, Jesus and disciples
Peace
Mission: to whom and for what?
Spirit
Sins
Believe and belief

Chapter 21
People present: named and unnamed
Time of day
Title used for disciples
Love
Mission: to whom and for what?
Glory/glorify
Testimony/witness

Selected Bibliography

Brown, Raymond. *The Community of the Beloved Disciple*. New York: Paulist, 1979.

———. *The Gospel According to John*. New York: Doubleday, 1966, 1970.

Bultmann, Rudolf. *The Gospel of John*. Philadelphia: Westminster, 1971.

Collins, Raymond. *These Things Have Been Written*. Grand Rapids, Mich.: Eerdmans, 1990.

Culpepper, R. A. *The Anatomy of the Fourth Gospel*. Philadelphia: Fortress, 1983.

Fortna, Robert. *The Fourth Gospel and Its Predecessor: From Narrative Source to Present Gospel*. Edinburgh: Clark, 1988.

Kysar, Robert. *The Fourth Evangelist and His Gospel*. Minneapolis: Augsburg, 1975.

———. *John, the Maverick Gospel*. Atlanta: John Knox, 1976.

Lindars, Barnabas. *The Gospel of John*. London: Oliphants, 1972.

Martyn, J. Louis. *History and Theology in the Fourth Gospel*. Nashville: Abingdon, 1979.

Schnackenburg, Rudolph. *The Gospel According to St. John*. New York: Crossroad, 1968, 1980, 1982.

Index

Andrew, 41

Baptism, 67–75, 78–79, 155;
 and blind man, 73–74;
 blood from the side of
 Jesus, 72–73; dialogue
 with Nicodemus, 68, 69,
 78; and Feast of Taber-
 nacles, 71–72, 73–74; and
 foot washing, 74–75; of
 John, 67–68; water bap-
 tism, 68–73, 78; water
 from the side of Jesus,
 71–72
Beloved Disciple, 35–36, 37–38,
 140–49; identity of,
 140–41; Peter and, 112;
 Resurrection, 112, 113–14,
 115, 116; *see also* specific
 topics, e.g.: Community;
 Gospel According to John
Blind man, 11, 27–29, 73–74
Brown, Raymond, 131, 140

Charismatic movement,
 150–51, 157
Charlesworth, James, 141
Christ. *See* Jesus Christ
Chytraeus, David, 87
Collectivism, 150, 151, 152, 153

*Community of the Beloved Dis-
 ciple, The* (Brown), 131,
 140
Community, 129–39, 145–48,
 153–58; diversity, 131;
 dualism, 131; groups
 within, 131–32; sectarian
 nature of, 130–31; "Johannine school," 129, 130;
 problems in, 133–34; and
 synoptic gospels, 135–36
Crucifixion, 96–101, 102–09,
 136; *see also* Passion
Culpepper, A., 141

Didache, 76, 87
Docetism, 133
Dualism, 134

Ego Eimi, 11–14, 32, 95; as title,
 18
Eschatology, 121–28; *see also*
 Salvation
Eucharist, 75–78, 79, 87, 155;
 and faith, 77–78; and miracle of the loaves, 76

Faith, 39–48, 51, 52, 55–56,
 155, 160; content of,
 43–44; and Eucharist,

77–78; and God the father, 40–41; and individuals, 41–43; and sacraments, 79

Feast of Tabernacles, 71–72, 73–74

Foot washing, 35, 74

Gnosticism, 47, 133, 134–35, 156

God: and faith, 40–41; as Father, 20, 103, 108; name of, 88; *see also* Jesus Christ; Paraclete

Good Shepherd, parable of, 41, 44–48, 50, 51, 52, 113, 130, 160

Gospel according to John: authorship of, 115, 140–41; eschatology, 121–28; farewell discourses, 82–92; historicity, 142–44; order of events, 136; prologue, 57–66; and synoptic gospels, 135–36; thematic guide, 160–68; *see also* specific topics, e.g.: Community; Salvation; Passion

Gospels. *See* Gospel according to John; Synoptic gospels

Grassi, Joseph, 140

Holiness, 89–90

Holy Eucharist. *See* Eucharist

Holy Spirit. *See* Paraclete

I am. See *Ego Eimi*

Individualism, 150–54; and Charismatic movement, 150–51; and Roman Catholicism, 151–53

James, William, 103

Jeremiah, 89

Jesus Christ, 7–19, 20, 137–38; birth of, 14–15; blood from side of, 72–73; death of, 102–9; divinity of, 8, 11, 14, 18, 19; glorification, 91, 99–100; holiness, 89–90; humanity of, 14–16, 18–19; and John the Baptist, 21–22; as messiah, 18–19, 22, 24, 35; self-offering, 103–05; as Son of Man, 9–10, 16–18; as Son of God, 10, 11; water from side of, 71–72; as Wisdom of God, 57, 79; as Word of God, 8, 9, 146; *see also* specific topics, e.g.: Passion; Resurrection

Jewish Christians, 132

Jews, 43, 132, 144, 160

Johannine community. *See* Community

John the Apostle. *See* Beloved Disciple

John the Baptist, 21–22, 42, 65, 67–68; and Jesus, 21–22; as messiah, 132, 133

John, Gospel of. *See* Gospel according to John

Judaism, 59; *see also* Jews

Judas, 31–32, 42

Kragerud, A., 141

Lame man, 27–29

Lazarus, of Bethany, 30–31, 125

Loaves, miracle of the, 76, 78

Logos, 9, 16, 58, 59; origin of, 58; *see also* Word of God

Love, 48–56, 82, 130, 155, 160;

of enemies, 49, 50, 130; and faith, 51, 155, 160

Luke, gospel of: Jesus as shepherd, 44; love of enemies, 49; sacraments, 78; words of Jesus, 146

Mark, gospel of: humanity of Jesus, 14; Jesus as shepherd, 44; Jesus as Son of Man, 16; sacraments, 78; words of Jesus, 146

Martha, 30–31, 125

Mary Magdalene, 33–34, 37; Resurrection, 112–13, 115

Mary, of Bethany, 30–31

Mary, the mother of Jesus, 32–33, 38

Matthew, gospel of: humanity of Jesus, 14; Jesus as shepherd, 44; Jesus as Son of Man, 16; love of enemies, 49; sacraments, 78

Memra, 59–60

Messiah, 18–19, 22, 24, 35

Miracles, 137; *see also* specific miracles, e.g.: Loaves, miracle of the

Moses, 89

Mysticism, 53–54

Name of God, 88

Nathaniel, 22–23, 42

Nicodemus, 23–24, 34, 42; and baptism, 67, 68, 69, 78

Paraclete, 83–85; and disciples, 84; functions of, 83; and future generations, 85; and world, 84

Passion, 93–101; Crucifixion, 96–101, 136; *ego eimi*, 13;

prayer of Jesus, 85–86; in synoptic gospels, 93–95; theme of exaltation, 97–98

Paul, 93, 126

Penance, 80

Peter, 35–36, 37, 112, 115

Philip, 29–30, 40–41

Philo, 59

Pilate, 96

Qumran, 134–35

Resurrection, 110–17

Roman Catholicism, 151–53

Royal official, 27

Sacraments, 67–81, 155; and faith, 79; *see also* Baptism; Eucharist

Salvation, 46, 47, 104, 107, 121–28

Samaritan woman, 24–26

Schmithals, W., 140–41

Schnackenburg, Rudolph, 140

Secret Identity of the Beloved Disciple, The (Grassi), 140

Shepherd, parable of. *See* Good Shepherd, parable of

Synoptic gospels, 48–49, 86–87, 135–36; Christology, 137–38; divinity of Jesus, 8; *ego eimi*, 13; Good Shepherd and flock, image of, 44; Gospel according to John and, 135–38; John the Baptist, 21; loaves, miracle of the, 76, 78; miracles, 137; order of entries, 136; parables, 48; Passion, 93–95; Peter, 35; Resurrection, 110–11, 112, 113; words of Jesus, 136–37;

see also specific gospels,
   e.g.: Mark, gospel of

Targums, 59, 60
Thomas, 34–35, 41, 114–15

Unity, 90–91

Vatican Council II, 152
Vine and the Branches, parable
   of, 41, 50, 51–52, 55

Wisdom, 57–58, 59, 60, 75, 79
Word, 8, 9, 60–65, 76, 138; ori-
   gin of, 58–59; see also
   Logos